NORTH AMERICAN BOWS, ARROWS, AND QUIVERS

NORTH AMERICAN BOWS, ARROWS, AND QUIVERS

An Illustrated History

Otis Tufton Mason

Skyhorse Publishing

www.skyhorsepublishing.com

10 9 8 7 6 5 4 3 2 1

Library of Congress Cataloging-in-Publication Data

Mason, Otis Tufton, 1838-1908.
  North American bows, arrows, and quivers : an illustrated history / Otis Tufton Mason.
    p. cm.
  Previously published: Yonkers, N.Y. : C.J. Pugliese, 1972.
  ISBN-13: 978-1-60239-115-4 (alk. paper)
  ISBN-10: 1-60239-115-7 (alk. paper)
  1. Indian weapons—North America. 2. Bow and arrow. 3. Indians of North America—Implements. I. Title.

E98.A65M3 2007
621.9'008997—dc22
                              2007017423

Printed in India

FOREWORD

When Otis T. Mason wrote *North American Bows, Arrows and Quivers*, which first appeared in "The Annual Report of the Smithsonian Institution" in 1893, it was probably the most comprehensive study on the subject of Native American archery ever published. Over a hundred years have passed since its initial publication, but it remains viable as a study on the subject, and even today few works surpass it. This book covers and discusses many of the native archery specimens in the Smithsonian collection and is lavishly illustrated with dozens of beautiful pen and ink line drawings which show details better than the photography of the day could have.

Dr. Mason held a long and distinguished career at the Smithsonian. He was one of those rare scholars who took great delight in his work and possessed a contagious enthusiasm for it. As early as 1872, he became interested in anthropological research work at the museum, and in 1874, he was made a collaborator in ethnology while still holding the position of principal at Columbian Preparatory School. For twelve years, when not teaching, he gave his time, energy, and attention to the collections by cataloging and arranging them in the museum's newly built halls. In 1884, he quit his teaching position and became head curator of the department of ethnology at the National Museum—a position he held for nearly a quarter of a century. Dr. Mason's interests covered a wide range of subjects in his field and he authored dozens of various papers and articles in anthropology especially relating to ethnology. This reprint of the 1893 edition of *North American Bows, Arrows, and Quivers* is only one of his many published works.

As an illustrator of a number of publications on Native American bows, arrows and quivers, and a student of the subject myself, I've often felt an affinity for this book's author and illustrator. I know well the toil involved to produce art work of this quality, because I have worked on many similar pen-and-ink illustrations. The quality of the illustrations in the Mason publication set a standard of excellence for me to follow while doing my illustrative work. I wish I could have met the man.

Dr. Bert Grayson—a well-known name in the realm of traditional archery and a man to whom I owe much thanks and gratitude—first introduced me to *Native American Bows, Arrows, and Quivers* in the early 1980s. I very much wanted a copy after seeing his, but I was never able to procure one for my library. Instead, I made a photocopied version, which is now dog-eared and falling apart from years of hard use. Needless to say I am delighted that this book is being published again. It is a must for anybody interested in Native American archery.

STEVE ALLELY
April 22, 2007

NORTH AMERICAN BOWS, ARROWS, AND QUIVERS.

By Otis Tufton Mason.

"If the canopy of Heaven were a bow, and the earth were the *cord* thereof; and if calamities were the arrows, and mankind the marks for those arrows; and if Almighty God, the tremendous and the glorious, were the unerring archer, to whom could the sons of Adam flee for protection? The sons of Adam must flee unto the Lord."—*Timur's Institutes*, p. xlviii.

In no series of museum specimens is the natural history of human invention better exemplified than in the apparatus of war and the chase. The history of warfare especially involves the right understanding of two words—offense and defense. The perfecting of defensive apparatus has been stimulated by the perfecting of weapons of offense, and on the contrary the ingenuity of the human mind has been taxed to make the offensive implement of war more powerful than the defensive. Protection of the body is secured by what is generally termed armor. The protection of the family, the tribe. the army corps, is achieved by fortification of some kind.

In the modern art of war this conflict of defense against offense reaches its climax in the built-up steel rifle-cannon and the nickel and steel Harveyized armor plating. One of the modern guns will send its shot quite through a plate 20 inches thick. Now the primitive form of this terrible projectile was the arrow, and of the steel plate the ancestor was the trifling hide and stick armor of savagery.

Offensive implements in all ages and stages of culture are for three purposes—to bruise, to slash, and to pierce the body of the victim.

Bruising weapons are found everywhere, but were highly developed in the Polynesian area, because there abundance of hard wood exists and little stone with conchoidal fracture for chipping.

Among the African savages, because they possess iron which may be worked from the ore, edge or slashing weapons have been especially elaborated.

Among the American aborigines, where obsidian, jasper in all its varieties, chert, quartz, and other siliceous stones abound, piercing weapons seem to have been the favorite class.

However, each of the chief types of savagery possesses in some form the three great classes of bruising, slashing, and piercing weapons. For instance, the Polynesians had the club, the spear, and the shark's-teeth sword. The Africans fought with knobsticks, assegais, bows and arrows, and edge weapons in great variety. The Americans, especially the Mexicans, developed a sword with obsidian edge and the tomahawk.

The further subdivision of these three classes of weapons is based upon their manipulation. Every weapon and every tool consists of two parts—the working part and the manual or operative part,—that which wounds or kills and that by which it is held or worked. Indeed, the fact is sometimes overlooked that the manual or operative part of a tool or weapon has undergone greater changes in the course of history than the working part. The bow therefore must be studied quite as carefully as the arrow.

In the rudest form of tool or weapon a single piece of stone or wood serves both purposes, but even in this simple form one part fits the hand better and the other is more adapted to the work. A stone used for bruising generally has one end better fitted to the hand and the other shaped by nature to effect the purpose. The stick used as a spear, or a club, or a sword, even in savagery, has the differentiation of holding end and working end.

This study of the manual end of a weapon gives rise to the classification of Adrien de Mortillet into weapons held and used in the hand, weapons thrown from the hand, and weapons worked by some intermediary apparatus between the hand and the working part.

Ballistic weapons of America are bolas, throwing-sticks or sling-boards with their varied darts, slings and stones, blow-tubes and darts, and bows and arrows. Some tribes are said to throw the tomahawk with good effect. Each of these involves mechanical principles worthy of the most careful study.

In this paper attention will be confined to the types of bows, arrows, and quivers of the North American aborigines, with incidental references to similar forms found elsewhere. It is true that the tribes included within this area developed the greatest variety of forms of primitive bows and arrows. The built-up bows of Asia, studied and described by Mr. Balfour,* are of a higher order of invention and need only be mentioned.

Mexican bows, arrows, and shields have been carefully described by Mr. Adolf Bandelier. The South American area has been little investigated, but the North American Indian archery affords an excellent opportunity for the consideration of all the forces and devices which entered into human inventions as motives.

The geographic distribution of materials for weapons and of game

---

* Henry Balfour, *Jour. Anthrop. Inst.*, London, vol. XIX.

has given rise to an infinite variety of forms. The failure of certain kinds of trees in many places has put the bowyers to their wit's end in devising substitutes for producing the bow's elasticity. The exigencies of climate and the gloved hand modify the form of the arrow in some regions. The progress of culture, the demands of social customs, and skill of the manufacturer enter into the study of the bow and the arrow. In other words, in passing from the Mexican border northward to the limit of human habitation, one finds the rudest arrow and the rudest bow and the most elaborate arrow and bow ever seen among savages.

Again, in making this journey he will observe how quickly his passage between certain isotherms, forested regions, deserts, tallies with a sensitiveness of the bow or the arrow, which take on new forms at every degree of latitude or temperature.

Finally, if the student be observant, the arrow will write for him long chapters about the people, the fishes, birds, and beasts of the separate regions and their peculiar habits.

The following scheme of weapons devised by M. Adrien de Mortillet is modified to fit the North American Area.

A.—BRUISING AND MANGLING WEAPONS

1. *Held in the hand.*—Stones, clubs.
2. *At end of handle.*—Pogamoggans and casse têtes.
3. *Thrown from hand.*—Sling stones, rabbit sticks, bolas.

B.—SLASHING AND TEARING WEAPONS.

4. *Held in hand.*—Stone daggers and swords.
5. *At end of handle.*—Sioux war clubs, tomahawks.
6. *Thrown from hand.*—Little used.

C.—PIERCING WEAPONS.

7. *Held in hand.*—Bone and stone daggers, slave killers.
8. *At end of handle.*—Lances of all kinds.
9. *Projectiles.*—Arrows, harpoons, blow-tube darts.

Besides those thrown from the hand—stones, rabbit sticks, and bolas—there were four types of manual or operative apparatus used for propelling missile weapons by the North American aborigines,—the bow, the throwing-stick, the sling, and the blow-tube.

The throwing-stick existed throughout the Eskimo area, in southeastern Alaska, on the coast of California and in Mexico. It is not necessary here to more than mention its occurrence in South America and Australia. This weapon has been described by the author at length in the report of the Smithsonian Institution (1884), and this paper was the starting point of half a dozen by others which well-nigh exhausted that subject.

The sling is found on the California coast north of San Francisco.

The blow-tube existed only in those areas where the cane grew in abundance, especially in the Southern States of the Union. One or two tribes of the Muskhogean stock and the Cherokees employ this weapon for killing birds in swampy places. The Choctaws about New Orleans make still a compound blow-tube by fastening four or five reeds together after the manner of the Pandean pipe. In Mexico and Central America this weapon was common. In tropical South America, however, much care was bestowed upon the manufacture of two varieties of Zarabatana constructed of two pieces of wood grooved and fitted together and the Pucuna made by inserting one tube inside of another and tamping the intervening places with wax.

From the inventor's point of view, the blow-tube with the dart, driven to the mark by the elasticity of the breath, should be the antecedent and parent of the gun, pistol, and cannon.* Historically the archer was the father of the cannonier. It is doubtful whether the inventors of gunpowder ever saw an American or Malayan blow-tube.

The universal projecting device of North America was the bow for propelling arrows and barbed harpoons. It is found in its simplest form in the south and east and becomes more complicated as we travel westward and northward. The following types are to be distinguished:

First. The plain or "self" bow, made of a single piece of hard, elastic wood, in each locality the best that could be found. (Plates LXI–LXIII.)

Second. The compound bow made of two or more pieces of wood, baleen, antler, horn or bone fastened together. (Plates LXII, LXIV, LXV.)

Third. The sinew-lined bow, consisting of a single piece of yew or other wood, on the back of which shredded sinew is plastered by means of glue. (Plates LXI–LXIII.)

Fourth. The sinew-corded bow used almost exclusively by the Eskimo. They are made from drift and other wood and backed with finely twisted or braided sinew cord and reinforced with wedges, splints, and bridges. (Plates LXV–LXXIII.)

Each one of these four types may be sub-divided according to the region or tribe. Every location furnishes a species of wood or material best suited for the bow-maker, and this has its effect upon the structure of the weapon. The game to be killed is another cause of variation. The tribal fashions, and material, and game, bring to pass a goodly number of special forms of bows which will now have to be studied in more detail, commencing at the south where the structure is simplest and proceeding to the north where it is most complex. Associated with each type and structure and region of the bow was its appropriate arrow. Nothing could be more intimate than this relationship. It might almost with safety be said that the arrows of each culture region could be shot with little effect from the bows of another region.

Again, excepting the little piercer at the end, which does the killing, the arrow shaft and feathers and nock really belong to the bow, that is, to the manual or operative part before mentioned.

---

* It is worthy of note, that *etymologically* "cannon," is a derivative from the Greek κ'ιννα—a reed.

VOCABULARY OF ARCHERY.

ARCHER, old French *archier*, Latin *arcarius*, from arcus, a bow; one who shoots with a bow; whence archery, shooting with a bow.

ARM-GUARD. The Japanese, in releasing, revolve the bow in the left hand; a guard is worn on the outer side of the forearm to catch the blow of the string.

ARROW, a piercing, stunning, or cutting missile shot from a bow. The possible parts are the pile or head, barb-piece, foreshaft, shaft or stele, feathering, nock, and seizings.

ARROW CEMENT, substance used in fastening the arrow-head to the shaft. A few tribes use glue or cement in making the sinew-backed bow.

ARROWHEAD, the part of an arrow designed to produce a wound. The parts of the primitive stone arrow-head are the tip or apex, faces, sides or edges, base, shank or tang, and facettes.

ARROW STRAIGHTENER, a piece of bone, horn, wood, or ivory, with a perforation to serve as a wrench in straightening arrow-shafts, barbs, etc.

BACK (side), the part of the bow away from the archer.

BACKED. A bow is backed when along the outside are fastened strips of wood, bone, horn, rawhide, baleen, sinew, or cord to increase the elasticity.

BALDRIC, the strap supporting a quiver or sheath, being worn over one shoulder, across the breast, and under the opposite arm; generally much ornamented.

BARB-PIECE, the piece of ivory, etc., on some arrows attached to the true head, and having barbs on the sides. This should be carefully discriminated from the foreshaft, which has another function altogether.

BASE of an arrow-head, the portion which fits into the shaft.

BELLY (inside), the part of a bow toward the archer, usually rounded.

BOW, an elastic weapon for casting an arrow from a string. (*See* Self-bow, compound bow, backed bow, grafted bow, built-up bow.) It is the manual part of the weapon.

BOW ARM, the arm holding the bow.

BOW CASE, a long bag or case of wood, skin, leather, or cloth, in which the bow is kept when not in use. Same as quiver.

BOW STAVE, the bow in a rough state. Bow-staves were an important item of commerce prior to the use of gun-powder and every thrifty Indian kept several on hand to work on at his leisure.

BOW-SHOT, the distance to which an arrow flies from a bow.

BOWSTRING, the string used in discharging a bow. The substances used, the method of treatment, and of nocking are important to notice.

BOW WOOD, the substances used for bows, generally wood, but horn, antler, bone, and metal have been employed.

BOWYER, a maker of bows. In many tribes these were professional bowyers.

BRACER (wrist-guard), a contrivance for protecting the archer's wrist from being galled by his bow-string.

BRACING (stringing), bending the bow and putting the eye of the string over the upper nock preparatory to shooting. The different methods of bracing throughout the world form an interesting study.

BUILT-UP BOW, one made by glueing pieces of elastic wood and other substances together, as in Asiatic examples (H. Balfour, *Jour. Anthrop. Inst.* vol. xix.)

BUTTS, pyramidal banks of earth used formerly for targets.

BUTT-SHAFT, a blunt arrow for shooting at a butt, the ancient style of target.

CHIPPING HAMMER, called also hammer stone, a stone used for knocking off chips or spalls in making stone arrowheads. There are really two kinds of these hammers, the hammer stone and the chipping hammer.

COCK-FEATHER, that feather of an arrow which is uppermost when the bow is drawn.

COMPOUND BOW, made of two or more pieces of wood, bone, antler, horn, or whalebone lashed or riveted or spliced together.

EYE, the loop of a bowstring which passes over the upper nock in bracing.

FACES, the broad, flat portions of an arrowhead.

FACETTES, the little surfaces left by chipping out a stone arrowhead.

FEATHERING, the strips of feather at the butt of an arrow, including the method of seizing or fastening.

FLAKER, the pointed implement of bone, antler, etc., used for shaping flint arrowheads, spearheads, etc., by pressure.

FLETCHER, and arrow maker, akin to *flèche*.

FOOTING, a piece of wood inserted in the shaftment of an arrow at the nock.

FORESHAFT, a piece of hard wood, bone, ivory, antler, etc., at the front end of an arrow to give weight and to serve for the attachment of the head or movable barb.

GRAFTED BOW, a species of compound bow formed of two pieces joined together at the handle or grip.

GRIP, the part of a bow grasped in the hand. The same term should be applied to the corresponding part of swords, daggers, etc., where it is differentiated in any manner.

GUARD (wrist guard), a shield of leather or other substance fastened to the wrist of the left hand to prevent injury from the bowstring (see bracer).

HORNS, the ends of a bow called also ears.

LIMBS, the parts of a bow above and below the handle or grip.

NOCK, properly the notch in the horn of the bow, but applied also to the whole of that part on which the string is fastened. Upper nock, the one held upward in bracing; lower nock, the one on the ground in bracing; also the notched part in the end of an arrow.

NOCKING, placing the arrow on the string preparatory to shooting.

NOCKING POINT, that place on a bowstring where the nock of the arrow is to be fitted, often whipped with silk.

NOOSE, the end of a string which occupies the lower horn of a bow.

OVER ARROWS, those shot over the center of the mark and beyond the target.

OVERHAND, shooting overhand is to shoot at the mark over the bow hand, when the head of the arrow is drawn inside of the bow.

PACKING, of leather, fish skin, or other soft substance used in binding the nocks and the grip of bows.

PILE, the head of an archery arrow; any arrowhead may bear the same name, in which case we have a one-pile, two-pile, three-pile arrow, etc.

PITCHING TOOL, or knapping tool, a column of antler or other hard substance, used between the hammer and the core in knocking off flakes of stone.

QUIVER. A case for holding the weapons of the archer—bow, arrows, fire-bag, etc.

REINFORCEMENTS, splints of a rigid material build into a compound or sinew-backed bow.

RELEASE, letting go the bowstring in shooting.

Prof. E. S. Morse characterizes the various releases as follows:

1. Primary release, thumb and first joint of forefinger pinching the arrow nock.
2. Secondary, thumb and second joint of forefinger, middle finger also on string.
3. Tertiary, thumb, and three fingers on the string.
4. Mediterranean, fore and middle fingers on the string.
5. Mongolian, thumb on string, with or without thumb ring.

RETRIEVING ARROW, one with a barbed head designed for retrieving fish or burrowing game.

RIBAND, a term applied to the stripes painted on arrow shafts, generally around the shaftment. These ribands have been called clan marks, owner marks, game tallies, etc.

SEFIN. (*See* Thumb ring.)

SELF BOW (simple), made of a single piece of wood or other material.

SHAFT, anciently an arrow, but strictly the portion behind the head, and in a fore-shafted arrow the lighter portion behind the foreshaft.

SHAFT GROOVES, furrow cuts along an arrow shaft from the head backward; they have been called blood grooves and lightning grooves, but these names are objectionable as involving theories of function little understood.

SHAFTMENT, the part of an arrow on which the feathering is laid.

SHANK, the part of an arrowhead corresponding to the tang of the sword blade.

SHORT ARROWS, those which fall short of the mark.

SIDES of an arrowhead, the sharpened portions between the apex and the base, also called the edges.

SINEW-BACKED BOW, one whose elasticity is increased by the use of sinew along the back, either in a cable, as among the Eskimo, or laid on solid by means of glue, as in the western United States. Wedges, bridges and splints are also used.

SLEIGHT, the facility with which an archer releases his bowstring.

SPALL, a large flake of stone knocked off in blocking out arrow heads.

STELE (stale, shaft), the wooden part of an arrow, an arrow without feather or head.

STRINGER, a maker of bowstrings.

TARGET, a disk of straw covered with canvas, on which are painted concentric rings, used in archery as a mark in lieu of the ancient butt.

THUMB RING, a ring worn on the thumb in archery by those peoples that use the Mongolian release; called sefin by the Persians.

TIP, a term applied to the sharp apex of an arrowhead.

TRAJECTORY, the curve which an arrow describes in space, may be flat, high, etc.

VENEER, a thin strip of tough, elastic substance, glued to the back of a bow.

WEIGHT of a bow, the number of pounds required to draw a bow until the arrow may stand between the string and the belly, ascertained by suspending the bow at its grip and drawing with a spring scale.

WHIPPING (seizing, serving), wrapping any part of a bow or arrow with cord or sinew regularly laid on.

WIDE ARROWS, those shot to the right or left of the mark.

Most of the words contained in this vocabulary stand for characteristics which are important in the study of bows and arrows according to natural history methods. By means of these terms any number of bows and arrows may be laid out so as to become types for all subsequent accessions and classifications. False information is thus eliminated, slowly, but the most scrupulous curator is not able to get rid of all that at once.

In all times the bow and the arrow have been the basis of much art and metaphor. Not only is this true in higher culture, as in the Bible, the Homeric poems, or the " arrow-head " writing of the Mesopotamians, but even among the North American Indians. The charming Ute ditty,

> The doughty ant marched over the hill
> With but one arrow in his quiver,

could easily be matched in other tongues. The Indians of the Southwest fasten an arrow dipped in blood on the bodies of their stone fetiches and call them the lightning. And Mr. Frank Cushing suggests that the positions of the elements in cuneiform writing are those of arrows dropped from the hand in divination.

THE BOW. *

In ancient times there was no other weapon into which a human being could throw so much of himself—his hands, his eyes, his whole mind, and body.† At any rate this is true of North America, where this arm was pre-eminent. In Polynesia and in Africa the case would be different. All of the early travellers in America speak of the sincere attachment of the warrior or the hunter to his artillery.

The noteworthy parts or characteristics of a bow are—

1. Back, or part of the bow away from the archer.
2. Belly, or part toward the archer.
3. Limbs, or parts above and below the grip. Also called arms.
4. Grip, or portion held in the hand.
5. Nocks, or ends upon which the bowstring is attached.
6. Horns, or parts projecting beyond the limbs, at the end are the nocks.
7. String, made of sinew, babíche or cord.
8. Seizing, application of string to prevent the splitting of the wood.
9. Backing, sinew or other substance laid on to increase the elasticity.
10. Wrist guard, any device to prevent the bow-string from wounding the wrist of the left hand.

Bows, as to structure, are—

1. Self bows, made of a single piece. Of these the horns may be separate.

2. Backed bows {
  with sinew {
    in a cable. Called sinew corded bows.
    glued on. Sinew lined bow.
    wrapped about. Seized bows.
  }
  with veneer   many kinds..
}

3. Compound.

Bows are to be studied also as to their materials, their shape, their strength, their history, and their tradition. (Plates LXI–XCV.)

In every Indian wigwam were kept bow-staves on hand in different stages of readiness for work. Indeed, it has been often averred that an Indian was always on the lookout for a good piece of wood or other raw material. This, thought he, will make me a good snow-show frame or bow or arrow and I will cut it down. These treasures were put into careful training at once, bent, straightened, steamed, scraped, shaped, whenever a leisure moment arrived. No thrifty Indian was ever caught without a stock of artillery stores.

Instances are on record where the wood for bows, the scions for arrows, the stones for heads, and even the plumage for the feathering were articles of commerce.

As a rule, however, the savage mind had as its problem, not that of the modern of ransacking the earth for materials and transferring them to artificial centers of consumption, but the development of the resources

---

* Consult Henry Balfour. " The Structure and Affinity of the Composite Bow," *J. Anthrop Inst.*, Lond., XIX; John Murdoch, A study of the Eskimo bows in the U. S. National Museum, Smithson. Rep., 1884, pt. ii; D. N. Anuchin, Bows and Arrows, Trans. Tiflis Archæol. Congress, Moscow, 1887; Lane Fox, Catalogue·

† Burton would claim this honor for the sword,

of each culture area, to make the bow and the arrow that each region would best help him to create. His was an epoch of differentiation.

"The rule laid down by the Apaches for making their bows and arrows was the following says Bourke:

"The length of the bow or rather of the string should be eight times the span from thumb to little finger of the warrior using it.

"The curvature of the bow was determined almost entirely by individual strength or caprice.

"The arrow should equal in length the distance from the owner's armpit to the extremity of his thumb nail, measured on the inner side of his extended arm; the stem should project beyond the reed to a distance equal to the span covered by the thumb and index finger. This measurement included the barb when made of sheet iron. The iron barb itself should be as long as the thumb from the end to the largest joint.

"Torquemada says that the Chichimecs, among whom he includes the Apaches, made bows according to their stature, a very vague expression. (*Mon. Ind. lib.*, XXI, introduction.)

"Gomara says that the Indians of Florida traen arcos de doce palmas. (*Hist. de las Indias*, 181.)

"Landa describes the Indians of Yucatan as making bows and arrows in the manner of the Apaches; La largura del arco es siempre algo menos que el que lo trae." (See *Cosas de Yucatan; Brasseur de Bourbourg*, Paris, 1864.*)

Baegert says the bows of the Lower California Indians were more than six feet long, slightly curved, and made from the root of the wild willow. The modern cottonwood bow, from the same region, is a long, clumsy affair, very near to the most primitive types. (Plate LXI, fig. 1.) The bow-strings were said to be made of the intestines of beasts. The shafts of arrows were common reeds straightened in the fire, six spans long, feathered, fore-shafted with heavy wood, a span and a half long, with triangular flint point.† (Plate XLI, fig. 2.)

Coville says that the Panamint Indians of Death's Valley, California, make their bows from the desert juniper (*Juniperus californica utahensis*). The Indian prefers a piece of wood from the trunk or a large limb of a tree that has died and seasoned while standing. In these desert mountains moist rot of dead wood never occurs. The bow rarely exceeds three feet in length and is strengthened by gluing to the back a covering composed of strips of deer sinew laid on lengthwise. The string is of twisted sinew or cord made from twisted hemp.‡

These Panamint belong to the Shoshonean stock, spread out over the Great Interior Basin, and all the tribes use the sinew-lined bow, with transverse wrappings of shredded sinew. (Plate LXI, fig. 4.)

The bow of the Chemehuevis (Shoshonean) is characteristic of the stock to which they belong, being of hard wood common in the region, elegantly backed with sinew and bound with shredded sinew, orna-

---

* Capt. J. G. Bourke, letter.
† *Smithsonian Report*, 1863, p. 362.
‡ *Am. Anthrop.*, Washington, 1892, vol. v, p. 360.

mented also at the end by the skin or rattle of the rattlesnake.* The type belongs to the stock everywhere.

"The Apache bow was made always of the tough, elastic mountain mulberry, called par excellence, 'Iltin,' or bow wood. Occasionally the cedar was employed, but the bows of horn, such as were to be seen among the Crows and other tribes of the Yellowstone region, were not to be found among the Apaches and their neighbors of Arizona.

"The elasticity of the fiber was increased by liberal applications of bear, or deer fat and sinew was, on rare occasions, glued to the back for the same purpose. †

It is not probable that any southern tribes of the family, to which the Apache belong, ever dwelt east of the Rocky Mountains. The Athapascan sinew veneered bow is found strictly west of the Rockies, the slender variety in the Basin and British Columbia, the flat variety on the Pacific Slope. The Navajo also have adopted this type of sinew-lined bow.

The Cherokees lived in the Piedmont portion of the Appalachians in Carolina, Georgia, and Tennessee. The finest oak, ash, and hickory abounds in this region. These tribes used every variety of available elastic wood for bows, the toughness of which they improved by dipping them in bear's oil and warming them before the fire.‡ The Cherokees were Iroquoian and their bows may be taken as the counterpart of those made by the Six Nations. The Algonquin bows were similar.

The Pawnee warrior always preferred a bow of *bois d'arc*, and besides the one in actual use he would often have in his lodge a stick of the same material, which at his leisure he would be working into shape as a provision against possible exigency. Bows of this wood were rarely traded away. *Bois d'arc*, however, was to be obtained only in the South, and for the purpose of procuring it a sort of commerce was kept up with certain tribes living there. §

The Blackfeet made their bows of the Osage Orange, but they were compelled to procure it by trade from the tribes down on the Arkansas River.‖ The Blackfeet are Siouan in language and dwelt in the buffalo country in northwestern Dakota. They were in the same mode of life as the Pawnees, who dwelt farther south and are of the Caddoan stock. The whole length of the Missouri River was traversed in this Blackfeet commerce. (Plate LXXXIV, fig. 2.)

The Central Eskimo, about Hudson Bay, have two kinds of bows (pitique), a wooden one (Boas's figs. 438 and 439, p. 502), and another made of reindeer antlers (Boas's figs. 440 and 441, p. 503). Parry gives a very good description of the former (II, p. 510):

"One of the best of their bows of a single piece of fir, 4 feet 8 inches in length, flat on the inner side and rounded on the outer, being 5 inches in girth about the middle, where, however, it is strengthened on the

---

* Whipple, etc., Pac. R. R. Rep., vol. III, p. 32, pl. 41, bow and quiver.
† J. G. Bourke, letter. Also J. G. Morice, Trans. Can. Inst., IV, 58.
‡ Timberlake, quoted by Jones, So. Indians, p. 252.
§ The Pawnee Indians, J. B. Dunbar.
‖ Maximilian's Travels, p. 257.

concave side, when strung, by a piece of bone 10 inches long, firmly secured by treenails of the same material. At each end is a horn of bone, or sometimes of wood covered with leather, with a deep notch for the reception of the string. The only wood which they can procure not possessing sufficient elasticity combined with strength, they ingeniously remedy the defect by securing to the back of the bow, and to the horns at each end, a quantity of small lines, each composed of a plat or "sinnet" of three sinews. The number of lines thus reaching from end to end is generally about thirty; but, besides these, several others are fastened with hitches round the bow, in pairs, commencing 8 inches from one end, and again united at the same distance from the other, making the whole number of strings in the middle of the bow sometimes amount to sixty. These being put on with the bow somewhat bent the contrary way, produce a spring so strong as to require considerable force as well as knack in stringing it, and giving the requisite velocity to the arrow. The bow is completed by a woolding round the middle and a wedge or two here and there, driven in to tighten it.

The bow represented in Boas's fig. 439, p. 503, is from Cumberland Sound and resembles the Iglulik pattern. The fastening of the sinew lines is different and the piece of bone giving additional strength to the central part is wanting. In Cumberland Sound and farther south wooden bows each made of a single piece were not very rare; the wood necessary for their manufacture was found in abundance on Tudjan (Resolution Island), whence it was brought to the more northern districts.

The bows which are made of antler generally consist of three pieces, a stout central one beveled on both ends and two limb pieces riveted to it. The central part is either below or above the limbs, as represented in Boas's fig. 440, p. 503. These bows are strengthened by sinew cord in the same way as the wooden ones, and generally the joints are secured by strong strings wound around them. A remarkable bow made of antlers is represented in Boas's fig. 441, p. 503. The grip is not beveled, but cut off straight at the ends. The joint is effected by two additional pieces on each side, a short stout one outside, a long thin one inside. These are firmly tied together with sinews. The short piece prevents the bow from breaking apart, the long one gives a powerful spring. The specimen figured by Boas was brought home by Hall from the Sinimiut of Pelly Bay, and a similar one was brought by Collinson from Victoria Land and deposited in the British Museum. The strings are attached to these bows in the same way as to the wooden ones."*   Plate LXIV, fig. 4; LXV, figs. 1, 2.

The compound Eskimo bow is found in a region where timber does not grow, where driftwood even does not come in such state as to be serviceable, and where whale, narwhal, caribou, and musk ox furnish

---

* *cf.* Franz Boas, The Central Eskimo, *Rep. Bur. Ethnol.*, vol. VI, pp. 502, 503.

ideal material for the purpose.   Last of all came the whaler with plenty of hoop wood, and the ship's blacksmith.   In the National Museum the material for the compound bow is baleen, antler, horn, ivory, and wood from whale ships.   The grip is the foundation piece, round and rigid. The limbs are worked to shape, spliced on to the ends of the grip and seized in place by a wrapping of sinew yarn or cord or sinnet.   The notches are cut on both sides of the nock, which is often pegged on to the end of the limb with treenails.   The whole class of projecting weapons must be looked upon as a lesson in techno-geography and as a remarkable example of the power of human ingenuity to throw off all precedents and predilections under sufficient stress and resort to those new methods which nature declares to be the only thing to do.

As previously intimated every Indian boy learned to make a bow. Every Indian man had a certain amount of skill in the art, and when he scoured about the forests, the capabilities of trees for his purposes engaged his thoughts.   He saved up good pieces for a rainy day and made the improvement of his artillery a pastime.   When he became old, if the fortunes of his existence accorded him such a doubtful blessing, he kept his hold on his tribe by becoming a bowyer when he could no longer take the field.   Since the substances used in making bows are of the region, techno-geography finds an excellent illustration in the study of the bows of North America, which may be on this basis thus divided:

(1) *The hard-wood, self-bow area*.   It embraced all North America east of the Rocky Mountains and south of Hudson Bay.   This area extends beyond the mountains along the southern border, and is invaded by the compound bow at its northeastern extremity.   Indeed, in those regions where more highly differentiated forms prevailed, it constantly occurs as the fundamental pattern.   (Plates LXI–LXIV, LXXX, LXXXI, LXXXIII–LXXXVI, LXXXIX.)

(2) *The compound-bow area*.   By the compound bow is meant one in which the grip and the two wings are separate pieces, or one in which the cupid's bow is made up of as many bits of horn as are necessary. There are really two compound-bow areas, the northeast Eskimo and the Siouan.   The former has been described by Boas.

The compound bows of the Sioux are made of buffalo and sheep horn and of the antler of the elk.   Dr. Washington Matthews states that he has seen a bow made of a single piece of elk horn.   All the examples examined by the writer are wrapped with flannel or buckskin so as to conceal every trace of the joints made by the union of the different parts.   The compound bows of the Sioux are the most beautiful in shape of any among savage tribes and recall the outlines of the conventional form of artists.   In both types the compound bow arose from a dearth of wood for making a self-bow.   (Plates LXII, LXIV, LXV.)

The horn bow was not confined to the parts of America inhabited by the great ruminants.　Pandarus' bow is thus described by Homer—

'Twas formed of horn, and smoothed with artful toil,
A mountain goat designed the shining spoil,
Who pierced long since, beneath his arrows bled,
The stately quarry on the cliffs lay dead,
And sixteen palms his brows large honors spread.
The workmen joined and shaped the bended horns,
And beaten gold each taper point adorns.

(Balfour in the work quoted has exhausted this theme.)

(3) *The sinew-lined bow area.*—By sinew-lined bow is meant one in which finely shredded sinew is mixed with glue and laid on so that it resembles bark.　This area extends up and down the Sierras in the western United States and British Columbia, on both slopes, and reaches as far north as the headwaters of the Mackenzie.　(Plate LXI.)

The occurrence of hard wood in the Great Interior Basin and of yew and other soft woods on the western slopes gives rise to the wide, thin bow in the latter, and the long, ovate, sectioned bow in the basin.

The Shoshonean or narrow bow occupies the interior basin, and is found also in the hands of Athapascans in Canada, and Apache, Navajo, and Pueblo tribes farther south.　Its chief characteristic, in addition to the ovate section, is that in many examples, at intervals of a few inches, after the back was laid on, it was wrapped with narrow bands of sinew.　These hold the backing to the wood and prevent splitting (Pl. LXI).　This device seems necessary with these narrow examples.　Scarcely one may be found an inch across the back, affording not enough sticking space for the glue.　With the broad California bows it was different.

(4) *The sinew-corded bow area.*—Where the bow has a backing made up of a long string or braid of sinew, passing to and fro along the back. This has been carefully studied and described by Murdoch.*

He divides the bows into classes, and shows how each of these classes originated, partly by the resources and exigencies of the environment and partly through outside influences.　There are practically four classes of this corded or laced pattern, to wit:

(a) *The Cumberland Gulf type.*—In these the sinew cord, or yarn, is made fast to one nock, and passed backward and forward along the back of the compound bow forty or fifty times.　In addition to this, additional strength is given by half turns and short excursions to and fro on the back of the grip.　Mr. Murdoch considers this the primitive type of the sinew-backed bow.　(Plates LXIV, LXV.)

(b) *The South Alaskan type.*—The bow is of wood, broad, flat, and straight, but narrowed and thickened at the grip.　The back is flat, and the belly often keeled, and frequently a stiffener of wood or ivory occurs under the sinew lining.　There is a subtype of this bow from

---

* *Report of U. S. National Museum,* 1884, p. 307–316.　Plates I–XII.

the Kuskoquim area, in which the ends bend backward abruptly, so as to lie along the string, as in the Tatar bow. In this type the strands of sinew cord lie parallel, pass entirely from end to end, and the last one is wrapped spirally around the rest. The whole of the broad part of the limbs is often seized down with spaced spiral turns of the cord. Next to the Cumberland type this is simplest, and is only a slight departure from it. (Plates LXV–LXVII.)

(c) *The Arctic type.*—The bow is shorter and narrower, the ends are often bent as in the Tatar bow, and strips of sealskin are put under the backing. The cord is always braided sinew, passes from nock to nock, but is laid on in a much more complicated manner, and much more "incorporated with the bow." The whole process of laying on the backing is minutely described by Mr. Murdoch. (Plates LXVIII–LXX.)

(d) *The Western type.*—Bow broader and flatter than the last, but less contracted at the grip, either straight or Tatar shape. The backing is in three parts, none of which extend as far as the nocks. The first cable goes from end to end near the nocks; the second from elbow to elbow, say a foot from each nock; the third along the straight part of the back. The cables become practically one along the grip. The method of laying down and knotting this intricate lashing must be studied from the figures (Plates LXXI, LXXII,) so that in the Eskimo area we have: (1) The plain or self-bow, of one piece; (2) the compound bow, of whalebone, antler, bone, ivory or wood; (3) the compound and sinew-corded bow; (4) the single-cabled straight bow; (5) the single-cabled Tatar or three-curved bow; (6) the complex-cabled straight bow; (7) the complex-cabled Tatar bow; (8) the three-cabled straight bow; (9) the three-cabled Tatar bow.

The material of bows varies geographically. Beginning in the south the regions may be roughly marked off—

(1) Mexican border: Cottonwood, willow, mezquit, bois d'arc, juniper.

(2) Southern United States: Hickory, oak, ash, hornbeam, walnut.

(3) Northeastern United States: Hickory, oak, ash, walnut, hornbeam, sycamore, dogwood, and, indeed, any of the many species of hard wood.

(4) Mississippi Valley: Same as on the Atlantic slope.

(5) Plains: Bois d'arc coffee tree and ash, wood procured in commerce.

(6) Interior basin: Mezquit in the south, abundant woods in the north, hard and elastic; species not determined.

(7) California and Oregon: Evergreen woods, yew, spruce.

(8) Columbia River: Same as California.

(9) Southeastern Alaska: Willow, spruce.

(9) Western Canada: Birch, willow, maple, spruce, cedar.

(10) Eskimo: Driftwood and timber from whale ships and wrecks.

The bow-string among the North American tribes was made of the following:

(1) Strips of tough rawhide plain or twisted.

(2) String made of the best fibers of the country—hemp, agave, etc.

(3) The intestines of animals cut into strips and twisted.

(4) But most frequently of sinew.

The strip of gristle extending from the head along the back and serving to support the former, and those taken from the lower part of the legs of deer and other ruminants were selected. These were hung up to dry. For making bow-strings the gristle was shredded with the fingers in fibers as fine as silk in some tribes, but coarser in others. These fibers were twisted into yarn on the thigh by means of the palm of the hand, after the manner of the cobbler. For making the twine some tribes employed only the fingers. Taking two yarns by one end between the tips of the thumb and forefinger extended of the left hand, the twister seized one yarn with his right hand, gave it two or three twists and laid it down on the palm of the left where it was kept in place by the fingers. Seizing the other yarn he repeated the process, brought it over the first yarn, laid it on the palm, caught the other yarn with the fingers of the left and seized the yarn first twisted with his right hand, all without losing a half turn. The writer has seen this work done with great rapidity. New strands of shredded sinew or vegetable fiber may be introduced at any time.

Both in New Mexico and in Alaska the natives make twine by means of a twister that works after the fashion of the watchman's rattle. But this device may be an innovation. The string of the Cherokee bow is said to have been made of twisted bear's gut.* The same material is mentioned in other connections east of the Mississippi River. There is a faint suspicion that in some instances the narrator mistakes the sinew cord for gut strings.

The study of the knots of savages is yet incomplete. Again many bows are sent to museums without strings, or unstrung, or falsely strung. The lower end of a bow-string, technically called the noose, was fastened on by the "timber-hitch," two half turns or hitches. There is no "eye," so called, wrought on the string, but the bow is strung by making two or more half hitches around the notches at the upper end. Neither is there any nocking point seizing on the bow-string of any American tribe.

The ancient bowyers made these ends of their bows of horn and trimmed and polished them in great fashion. Many examples from the Malayan and the Papuan area have the extremities very daintily carved. But the American bow has nothing approaching this. In a few Oregon examples the sinew backing is at the extremities gathered up in a hornlike extremity and finished off with fur, beads, and the like.

---

* Jones, So. Indians, 252.

Otherwise the end of the bow stave is rounded, cut in on one side or on two for the bow-string.

It was not the custom to apply a "packing" or a woolding on the grip of bows. The eastern tribes did not. But the compound bow of the Sioux, the flat yew bows of the California tribes, and the ellipsoidal sinew-backed bow of the Shoshonean tribes, were so treated. In addition to this, in many cases, the bows were painted in several colors, geometric figures were marked on them, and additions of bead-work made them quite fine. This decoration of the bow occurs among west coast tribes that manifest extraordinary artistic tastes in baskets and other work.

The warrior and the hunter tended their bows with as much care as though they were children. Every time they were used they were careful to oil them in order to preserve their elasticity. The western Eskimo wound up his bow when he desired to use it, and was careful to unwind and straighten it as soon as the hunt was over. This winding was done by twisting the sinew cable along the back by means of ivory levers making only a half turn, and then sliding their whole length through the cable before repeating the process. The ordinary self-bow when not in use was straightened and pushed into the bow case. (Plate XCIII.)

The author can find little authentic information concerning the bracing of the bow by the North American Indians. Those that he has seen perform the operation followed the old English method, placing the bottom horn against the hollow of the left foot, holding the upper horn in the left hand, bending the bow with the left knée, and tying the bowstring with the right hand. There was usually no eye in the bowstring that slid down on the bow and pushed up into the nock in bracing.

Frequent reference is made to the bracer or wrist guard of the North Americans. In the far north the gloved hand and the long sleeve made such device almost unnecessary, but a few specimens of carved bone or ivory objects in collections from the hyperborean area bear that name. The Indian, par excellence, wore upon his left wrist a band of rawhide, from 2 to 3 inches wide, as a guard against the bowstring. Many of these come from the Southwest, where they are ornamented with silver and worn in ceremonies.

"Among the Yurok bows and arrows were made by old men skilled in the art."* As will be seen further on in studying the arrow, there was really no guild or craft of bowyers. In his childhood the Indian made the best bow he could. Whatever ingenuity he expended upon it yielded him an immediate patent. He not only had the exclusive use of it, but every improvement which he made upon it inured to his advantage at once in the form of sustenance, flattery, and substantial social reward.

---

* Powers, *Cont. to N. A. Ethnol.*, vol. III, p. 152.

So far as known the savages of America were right-handed. But there is nothing in any bow from the northern portion of the continent to show this fact. Left-handed archery was certainly quite uncommon. In a large number of darting boards or throwing sticks, which under certain technical exigencies are used by the Eskimos in place of the bow, there are only two specimens that are left-handed. Among the women of the same areas, not one implement has been found fitting the left hand.

The conditions of sending an arrow into the vital part of any game are distance, wind, varying elasticity of the bow, varying weight of the arrow, proper shape of the weapon, penetrability of the game. Each one of these variables is rendered as constant as possible by the hunter, in skulking, getting to windward, using wood of the greatest strength for bows, and making one's own arrows. The intellectual stimulus in the creation and using of the bow and arrow was incalculable.

Oliver Marcy gives the following on arrow penetration:

" I have in my possession the sixth dorsal vertebra of a buffalo, the spine of which contains an iron arrow point. The arrow struck the spine about 2 inches above the center of the spinal canal, and penetrated the bone 0·82 of an inch. The bone at the point struck is 0·55 of an inch thick, and the point of the arrow protrudes beyond the bone 0·27 of an inch. The arrow was shot from the right side of the animal and the plane of the point was horizontal. The animal was mature and the bones well ossified. Though the vertebra has been much weathered, the epiphyses adhere closely. The animal was not as large as some individuals. The whole vertical length of the vertebra is 13 inches.

"The arrow must have penetrated several inches of flesh before striking the bone." *

He does not take into consideration also the thick hide and matted woolly hair, both especially thick at the point struck.

As it is customary in rating the stature of a people to disregard the giants and the dwarfs, so in rating the North American projectile we may as well omit the marvellous and exceptional successes in company with the egregious shortcomings in order to know the importance of the average. When these allowances are made, there is enough to show that for accurate and rapid and effectual shooting the bow and arrow in the hands of a skilled warrior or hunter were a creditable weapon. The distance at which an Indian bow will do execution has not been studied among the tribes. As previously said, the design of the hunter or the warrior was to get close up. In all the sham battles which the writer has witnessed from his boyhood, the warriors almost touched each other. The dexterity with which they parried and fenced with the arm shield and the bow and arrow was marvellous. The absence of noise, the invention of game drives, the universality of decoys, the hundreds of disguises, the efficient skulking, the imitations of the cries of animals, all point to the intention of getting within a distance of 20 yards or less.

---

*Science, vol. VII, p. 528.

The South American weapon is half as long again and may do better farther off.

At the request of the author the president of the Washington Archery Club, Mr. Maxon, made experiments in the penetrating power of Indian arrows and the propulsive power of Indian bows. The result was that the self or plain bows are not equal to the best archery bows. But the sinew-backed bows of the Pacific coast were capable of as great execution as man is capable of making.*

"Constant practice," says Capt. John G. Bourke, "had made the Apaches dextrous in the use of the bow, arrow, and lance; their aim was excellent, and the range attained was perhaps as much as 150 yards. I am able from my own recollection to supply a number of illustrations of the great force with which the arrow was discharged, although a person observing for the first time an arrow coming toward him would be surprised at its apparent lethargy.

"In the summer of 1871 I was riding by the side of Gen. Crook on the summit of the elevated plateau known as the Mohollon Mountains, in Arizona. We were a short distance ahead of a large column of cavalry and our immediate party was quite small. We ran into an Apache ambuscade. A number of arrows were discharged, two of them piercing pine trees to a depth of at least 6 inches. On another occasion a pine door three-eighths of an inch thick was penetrated. In July, 1870, a friend of mine, M. T. Kennedy, was mortally wounded by an Apache arrow which pierced his chest. The autopsy disclosed the fact that the arrow had no head."

"Mackenzie speaks of having driven a headless arrow 1 inch into a pine log on the Columbia River in 1793. (See *Voyages*, London, 1800, p. 269.)

"Maltebrun speaks of the force with which the Apaches shot their arrows. 'At a distance of 300 paces they can pierce a man.' (*Univ. Geog.*, art. 'Mexico,' Eng. translation, Philadelphia, 1832, vol. III, lib. or cap. 85th, p. 293.) I doubt this very much, as in my own experience I have limited their range to 150 yards.

"Cabeza de Vaca seems to have been greatly impressed with the dexterity of the Indians seen along his route from Florida to the Pacific coast settlements. He tells us that with their arrows they could pierce through oaks as thick as a man's thigh; that the range of the arrow was 200 paces; that Spaniards had been transfixed by arrows notwithstanding that they wore good armor. (In *Ternaux*, vol. VII, p. 107.)

"Don Antonio Espejo also asserts that the wild tribes living in the drainage of the Rio Grande could pierce a coat of mail with their arrows. (*See* his 'Relacion,' in Hakluyt, vol. III, 460, p. 461, A. D. 1581.)

"Domenech says that the Indians have trials of skill with arrows and will often keep ten in the air at one time. (*Deserts*, vol. II, p. 198.) Refers

---

* For the contest between bow and musket, in 1792, at Pacton Green, Cumberland, and also at Chalk Farm, at 100 yards, *see* Hansard, vol. IX, p. xiii.

to Apache arrows sunk up to the feathers in the giant cactus on the side of the Santa Catalina Canyon in Arizona, 1870."*

Marvellous stories are told of the precision with which the American Indian could shoot. Cockburn said that the Indians of Darien could strike down with arrows the smallest flying bird. By shooting upward they were said to cause an arrow to pin a bird feeding on the ground. Sticking a shaft in the ground, they would shoot upward and the descending arrow would split the one sticking in the ground.†

The use of the bow was a part of the education of a boy. Among the many hundreds in the National Museum a great number are marked "boy's bow." In handling them the student must often speculate on the deferred breakfast that hung on the action of these miniature implements. We are told also that boys were frequently called out to shoot for prizes. That was the predecessor of all manual training schools, wherein skill and support went hand in hand with the Indian lad. Indeed, their games and pastimes were spirited imitations of the successes of their elders.

The author is not able to obtain reliable information as to whether the American tribes shot always "overhand"—that is, over the bow hand, with the arrow drawn inside the bow. Dr. Shufeldt, in his practical experiments to ascertain the mode of arrow release among the Navajos, incidentally remarks that the arrow was on the left side of the bow and rested on the top of the hand. In many descriptions, however, the forefinger is described as surrounding the arrow shaft.

At present the bow and the arrow have well nigh disappeared from the face of the earth as an active weapon. Four hundred years ago it stood in the forefront, where it had remained during thousands of years. It might be properly questioned whether, in the long run, the arrow had not destroyed more human lives than the bullet. In Canada, and sparingly elsewhere, bow guns or rude arbalests are found in the hands of Indians, but they are without doubt introduced. The arrow, having reached its highest elaboration as such in America, was superseded by the musket of the Aryan race.

The Iroquois tribes were among the first to receive firearms from the early settlers. On this account they soon abandoned the bow and the arrow. Colden says that they had entirely laid them aside in his day (1727). This abandonment of the bow for the gun has been spoken of as showing the Iroquois to have been a progressive people. Certain it is that this prompt adoption of the firearm put this confederacy at once at the head of the eastern Indians and made them a terror to the Algonquian tribes.

The almost entire absence of noise in the movement of the arrow and the shooting of the bow is the greatest differentiation from the gun, which alarmed the whole earth, man and beast. It may be said that

---

* Capt. J. G. Bourke, letter.   † Hansard, p. 26.

the noise of the gun put the man or beast to be killed quite as much out of the reach of that weapon as the little alarm created by the archer had moved the victim away from his weapon.

THE ARROW.

" The ancient arrow-maker
Made his arrow-heads of sandstone,
Arrow-heads of chalcedony,
Arrow-heads of flint and jasper,
Smooth and sharpened at the edges,
Hard and polished, keen and costly."

LONGFELLOW.

The continent of America furnishes excellent facilities for the study of the arrow. Every variety of climate, material, and land or water game are here, to create an indefinite diversity of structures.

In its simplest form, the arrow is a straight rod pointed at one end, perhaps in the fire, and notched at the other end for the bow-string. But such a missile would be of little worth; and so the arrow has undergone many modifications in answer to the demands of the hunter. The parts of a highly developed arrow are the following:

(1) The shaft; of which it is necessary to study the material, the technique, the form, the length, the grooves, and the ornamentations.

(2) The shaftment; which is that part of the shaft upon which the feather is fastened. This section of the arrow varies in length, in form, and greatly in ornamentation, because it is the part of the weapon upon which bands and other ornamental marks are usually placed.

(3) The feathering; or the strips of feather or other thin material laid on at the butt of the arrow to give it directness of flight. The study of this feature includes the method of seizing; the attaching to the shaftment; the position of the feather, whether flat or perpendicular to the shaft; the manner of trimming the plume; the line, whether straight or spiral, upon which each feather is laid, and the glue or cement.

(4) The nock; or the posterior end of the arrow, seized by the fingers in releasing. This is a very important feature in the study of this weapon. For instance, the Eskimo arrows have flat nocks, while all other arrows in the world seem to be more or less cylindrical or spherical. In some the form is top-shaped; in others, bulbous; in others, cylindrical; and in others, spreading, like the tail of a fish or swallow. In modern arrows a footing is added to the nock.

(5) The notch; or cut made at the end of the arrow to receive the bowstring. Each stock of aborigines has its own way of making this cut at the end of the arrow; and this characteristic, born of the material, though seemingly unimportant, is frequently helpful to the student in deciding upon the tribe to which the arrow belongs.

(6) The foreshaft; or that piece of hard wood or bone or ivory or antler laid into the anterior portion of the shaft and trimmed to a symmetrical shape. It serves the double purpose of making the front

of the arrow heavier than the rear, and also affords a better means of attaching arrow-heads or harpoon barbs of special form.

(7) The head; or that anterior part of an arrow which makes the wound or produces the result. Before contact with the white race, aborigines were wont to make their arrow-heads of stone, bone, wood, shell, and even of cold hammered metal. The study of the arrow-head involves the point or blade, the faces of the blade, the facettes and serrations and notches of the expanding blade, the butt or tang for attachment, the barbs, and sometimes the barb piece, which is an extra bit of bone or other substance fastened to the posterior end of the stone head to multiply the number of barbs. (Plate LV, figs. 2, 3.)

Now, each one of these parts may be varied in number, in form, in material, in artistic finish; or one or more may be wanting. It will be seen therefore at once what an excellent instrument the arrow may be for the study of the natural history of invention, how it has been influenced by climate and by material resources, how it has been modified for definite functions, and has developed complexity with age.

It will readily be seen from an examination of the foregoing analysis that the creation of an arrow involves a great many of our modern crafts. In every locality the arrow-maker has shown, first of all, a wonderful acquaintance with the materials at hand, as though he had searched all the resources of the mineral, vegetable, and animal world, and after studying all there was, had selected the best. We are not able now to discover that the savage could have found any better material within his own environment. For the selection and creation of the shaft there was demanded a knowledge of the best kind of woods, and the invention of knives, straightening apparatus, "sandpaper," dyeing apparatus, and glue or cement of some kind. In fastening the various parts of the arrow together sinew was employed. The savage stripped from the leg or the neck of one of the larger mammals a mass of sinew which he allowed to dry. It was then carefully pounded and shredded. When he was ready to use this material he placed several of the strips or fillets in his mouth until they became thoroughly soaked with saliva. Then, holding with his left hand the parts to be attached and one end of the sinew fillet, he held the other part of the sinew in his right hand and revolved the arrow shaft with the left, holding the parts still together until one or two turns were made. He could then use the fingers of his left hand in smoothing down the sinew and directing its course, while with the right he held the unwound portions tight and directed the sinew to its position. When the wrapping or seizing was nearly finished the loose end was carefully drawn under the last turn or two, pulled tight, and cut off, so that neither end was visible. The whole was carefully rubbed down and allowed to dry. The sinew in drying shrunk very much and bound the parts firmly together. (Plate I, fig. 6.)

The feathers of the arrow are usually taken from the wing or tail feathers of rapacious birds, though others are sometimes used. The feather is carefully split from one end to the other, and the pith and unnecessary parts of the quill carefully removed, so as to leave the plume and only a strip of the midrib. In laying the feather upon the arrow-shaft differences of manipulation existed among the different tribes. In some of them the midrib was laid close to the shaftment and glued tight, while the ends were seized with sinew, and the plume was shorn either very close to the shaftment in a parallel line or into some other artistic form. Not only the knowledge of birds was necessary in the choice and the arrangement of the feather, but there was a great deal of mythology connected with the proper bird whose feathers should be placed upon the arrow and the position and seizings connected with the feathering. (Plates XL–LX.)

The manufacture of the head of the arrow and its various parts involves knowledge of bone, ivory, or horn, and also familiar acquaintance with stone and stone-working. Arrowheads differ from one another in material, in size, in form, and in methods of attachment. The savage arrow-maker was a mineralogist. He not only knew the qualities of rocks but also their best methods of working, as well as the best conditions in which they existed for his purposes in nature. In each country the material employed is in every case the best from that region. In a large collection from the United States arrow-heads have been made of every variety of quartz, chalcedony, agate, jasper, hornstone, chert, novaculite, slate, argillite, and obsidian. In rare cases even quartz crystal, carnelian, amethyst, and opal were used. In working these materials the savage inventor soon found that the physical properties and availability of the material changed by natural surroundings. He knew by experimentation that a stone lying in a brook yielded him better results than one exposed to the sun and the weather on the open fields, and that a bowlder buried in the damp earth where it has lain for many centuries gave him safer results with less work than the brook pebble, so that he not only became a critical expert in the qualities of materials, but also was led to become a quarryman in order to exploit the proper materials. It has been very well shown by Professor Holmes that many spots supposed to have been the refuse heaps of Indian camps for many years, are only the sites of of ancient stone quarries, and the pieces found buried in these heaps are the refuse of their manufacture. In places the necessary rock could not be found in bowlders either on the surface or in the streams or in the gravel beds, but the materials were part of ancient ledges under ground, as in Ohio, Arkansas, and other places. It was necessary there to remove the surface soil, to dig out great pits, and by means of sledges and fire and other means within the capabilities of this Indian workman, to detach cores and masses of material which could be subsequently worked up into arrow-heads and other implements. As soon as the arrow-maker had secured his stock he began to work it up into the shape desired, first, with a stone hammer, by means of which he knocked off flakes or spalls of the proper size and shape. Sometimes he would introduce between his stone hammer and the block of material a "pitching tool" of antler or hard bone. As soon as the flake of proper dimensions was removed, the next thing with the artist was to bring this into proper form by means of the flaking tool or flaker. The method of dressing the chip of flint into shape varied from tribe to tribe; in some the pressure was downward; in others it was upward; and the method of holding the hand and doing the work will be described under the head of "arrow-makers' tools." Arrow-heads are frequently confounded with spear-heads and knife or dagger-blades. The smallest objects of this class are usually arrow-heads, and the size alone would decide in many cases, because, after reaching a certain weight, the blade would defeat its own purpose by being any larger. But there is no difference in shape between the arrow-head and the other objects mentioned. A great deal of attention has been paid to the forms of arrow-heads, but they may be reduced to a few simple classes, such as the leaf-shaped, either complete or truncated; the triangular, and the stemmed. Sub-divisions of these classes have been formed by archeologists, but many of these are such as have resulted from the limitations of the material in the hand of the artist. He has simply made that particular form because the material would yield to that and no other. Prof. Thomas Wilson, in classifying the arrows in the National Museum, mentions those, first, with beveled edges, the bevel being in one direction; second, with serrated edges; third, with bifurcated stems; fourth, with long barbs at the ends; fifth, triangular in section; sixth, broadest at the cutting end; and, seventh, all polished arrows.

As will be seen in the general and special descriptions of arrows, other substances besides stone were used for the heads. In the north and among the Esquimauan stock, frequently bone, ivory, antler, horn, and wood are found taking the place of stone. In each case that material was selected which would bring about the best results. For instance, what is called the "rankling" arrow, for the destruction of the reindeer, has its head made from the leg bones of the deer, the barbs upon the side are very sharp, and the dowel, for the insertion into the shaft of the arrow, very small, so that when the animal is struck the head would easily come out of the shaft and at every movement of the victim be carried further in toward its vital parts. Coming southward along the Pacific Slope, slate replaces chipped stone, and for barbed arrows native copper, bone, and wood are used. A few arrows from this region have also heads of shell. Along the Rocky Mountain slopes, in the land of the buffalo, before the days of iron heads, bone was used quite as often as stone in the fabrication of arrow-heads. Very few specimens are preserved in our museums of arrows from the tribes of the Eastern States, but historians convince us they were not different from their Western relatives in the material and form of their arrow-heads. Of the ancient inhabitants of this continent the perishable material of arrows constituting the shaft and other parts has rotted and left us naught but the stone heads. Even those of bone and wood and other material have passed away, so as to leave the impression that the Indians of this eastern region used only stone; but all authorities agree that other substances were employed quite as frequently as the last named.

There are as many ways of classifying arrows as there are parts of the arrow, and more, some important parts furnishing several classific concepts. These will be set down as they occur without regard to order, each time seeking to exhaust the arrow.

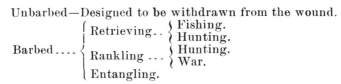

```
Unbarbed—Designed to be withdrawn from the wound.
            ┌ Retrieving.. ⎰ Fishing.
            │              ⎱ Hunting.
Barbed....  ┤ Rankling ... ⎰ Hunting.
            │              ⎱ War.
            └ Entangling.
```

The concept here is especially the existence and function of the barb, rather than number and structure of parts.

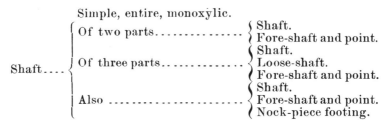

```
         Simple, entire, monoxylic.
         ┌ Of two parts............. ⎰ Shaft.
         │                           ⎱ Fore-shaft and point.
         │                           ⎰ Shaft.
Shaft....┤ Of three parts.......... ⎰ Loose-shaft.
         │                           ⎱ Fore-shaft and point.
         │                           ⎰ Shaft.
         └ Also ................... ⎰ Fore-shaft and point.
                                     ⎱ Nock-piece footing.
```

As to the feathering, arrows are (1) without feather; (2) two feathered; (3) three or more feathered; and, as to the attachments, (1) glued to the shaft; (2) fastened only at the ends; (3) with the quill inserted at its ends into the arrow shaft. The nock of American arrows are (1) flat as in the hyperborean zone; (2) bulbous or spread, as in Canada and North United States; (3) cylindrical, as in California and the southern tier of States. (Plates XL–LX.)

There are innumerable references to ancient arrow-makers among the North American Indians, but the probability is that the life history of the bowyer is repeated in that of the superannuated fletcher. First comes the boy struggling through his primitive institute of technology, then the warrior or hunter, skillful in making an arrow and in wearing it out. Last of all he takes the wings of Hermes from his feet and spends his closing years in making arrows for his sons.

There was, according to Chippewa tradition, a particular class of men among our Northern tribes, before the introduction of firearms, called makers of arrow-heads. The same is related by other Algonkians.* Longfellow's ancient arrow-maker will occur to every reader at once.

The operations of constructing one of the more elaborate American

---

* Schoolcraft, S. Rp., vol. III, p. 81.

arrows led a man into many trades—quarryman, stone-cutter, mineralogist, sinew-dresser, and wood-worker. In the far North he must be
also worker in bone, ivory, and horn. As a rule, in all savagery, both
with men and women, the user of an implement must be its manufacturer. Yet, the differentiation of trades is a necessary step in the
progress of culture, and our Indians had taken it more than once.

The North American savages were excellent quarrymen. In every
region they knew the very best kinds of siliceous stones, the very best
places to find these stones, the natural conditions under which they
were kept in the most fracturable state, the best way to break, flake,
and chip each stone into the desired shape.* The Indian was also a
good lapidary, as numerous sites examined by Holmes will attest.

Arrow-heads are found in immense numbers about the fields and along
the banks of rivers in the United States. It would not be an error to
say that they are numbered by millions. They occur in great abundance
upon the sites of ancient camps, near shell-heaps, fishing grounds, and
about the fields where used to wander the deer and other game sought
by the Aborigines. This is evidence that the making of an arrow-head
was an easy matter, while the shaft required much time and patience
to finish.

It has been said that by means of the stone, the shape and artistic
skill with which it is wrought, the edges, the tang, and the conse-
quent attachment to the shaft, arrows differ from tribe to tribe and
individual makers show certain idiosyncrasies in the same tribe. Chert,
slate and ivory in Eskimo land, wood and bone along the volcanic
portions of the Pacific Slope, in British Columbia and Alaska; the
most beautiful heads in the world of obsidian and jasper series in
Oregon and California, coarser stone in the East at once proclaim
what kind of arrows this or that tribe used.

According to Holmes the stages in making an arrowhead are fracturing, chipping, flaking. Fracturing is done at the quarry or wherever the
original stone is picked up. The simplest fashion is breaking one stone
with another; but stone from a quarry works better than surface bowlders. When the workable stone was in masses the Indian had more convenient tools, stone hammers or sledges, picks of wood or antler, and even
fire if he had need of it. The first operation is to break up the original
bowlders or masses so as to get out of its interior spalls capable of
being wrought into blades. Each kind of stone had its own best way
of treatment, whether quartz, quartzite, rhyolite, chert, agate, jasper,
chalcedony, obsidian, or what not. There did not exist in the United
States so pliable a form of flint as that occurring in great abundance
in western Europe. Obsidian and jasper gave the best results.

Chipping was also done with a hammer, but, this time, a pebble of
hard stone, oblong, convenient for the thumb and two fingers, and

* See W. H. Holmes, *Am. Anthropologist*, vols. v., vi.; J. C. McGuire, *id.*, vol. v.; H.
C. Mercer, *Pop. Sc. Month.*

somewhat bluntly pointed. The writer has often seen arrow-makers hold a spall of stone in the left hand between the thumb and closed fore finger, and by means of a dainty hammer stone knock off flakes with the greatest rapidity, barely touching the edge of the spall at each blow. Arrow-heads for common use may be finished by this means. (Plate I.)

The flaking of blades was done with a flaker. The simplest form of the flaker is a piece of bone from the leg of a deer, pointed at one end. The essential characteristics of the working end of this tool are that it be stout enough to stand any amount of pressure that a man can give, and that it be of such a texture that it will "take hold" of the stone. The outer side of antler, hard bones from the legs of ruminants, and even soft iron are excellent, but ivory or steel are not good materials for flakers. (Plate I.)

The Eskimo* make the best flakers, working the point from antler of the caribou and the handle from ivory, carving the latter to fit the hand and to give to the workman the best "purchase." The point is set in the end of the handle and firmly lashed in place by means of rawhide.

All tribes do not use the flaker similarly. If the reader will take a tooth-brush handle in his right hand and a chip of siliceous stone in the other, he may try the following methods:

(1) Lay the spall or chip on a table or bit of wood, holding it firmly in place with the left thumb and forefinger. Grasp the tooth-brush firmly in the right hand, with the thumb on the top. The handle will work better if it be sharpened like a husking peg. Press down the point near the edge of the spall firmly, and remove chips along the under side.

(2) Lay the chip on the palm of the left hand gloved, or upon a bit of rawhide, holding it in place with the fingers, but not the thumb. Press off flakes along the edge of the chip.

(3) Grasp the chip between the thumb and forefinger, so that its outer edge will lie along the ball of the thumb. Hold firmly with fingers and press off flakes toward the thumb.

In all cases the operator needs confidence and knack. Wonderful results are achieved by good workmen in such brittle material as bottle glass, obsidian, and the jaspers.

There are in Washington several men connected with the Bureau of Ethnology who are capable of producing the most beautiful arrow-heads from bits of obsidian or glass.

Within the past year or two a new light has been thrown upon the whole operation of arrow-head-making. Extensive ancient quarries have been opened in Washington City, Ohio, Pennsylvania, Minnesota, Arkansas, and the processes revealed. There were several steps followed certainly by the eastern fletcher.†

(1) The digging of moist stone from the quarry.

---

* Murdoch, IX, *An. Rep. Bur. Ethnol.*, pp. 288, 289.
† See Holmes, *Am. Anthropologist*, vols. V and VI.

(2) The making of blanks on the spot.

(3) The finishing by the processes named.

The arrow-maker among the Virginia Indians, for making his shafts, used a knife with a blade of beaver tooth set in a wooden handle. This served him for saw, knife, and chisel. John Smith tells us that he made the notch in his arrow-shaft by grating with this knife. For chipping his arrow-heads of stone he used "a little bone, which he ever weareth at his bracer, or any splint of a stone or glasse in the forme of a hart." The arrow-head was fastened to the shaft with deer sinew, held firm by means of a glue made of the tops of deer horns boiled to a jelly. This method is not unlike that of the Apache, Utes, and other tribes of the great interior basin.*

This is a charming connecting link between the prehistoric and the historic. The knife with a blade of beaver tooth may at this very day be seen in the hands of the Eskimos about the Yukon mouth. One could say that a grip or handle of wood or antler had a groove sunk into one end, the root of the tooth was laid in this, and the two lashed with wet rawhide. At present the Eskimos use their beaver-tooth knife to put a fine edge on their blades of steel. The front enamel of the tooth is so much harder than the rear that it makes a perfect chisel, and would act well for knife or saw. "The little bone that he weareth at his bracer" for flaking his arrow-heads one might see any day in the hands of a Ute warrior a few years ago, and Maj. Powell collected and deposited several in the National Museum. This is simply a little bit of the fibula of the deer. On the west coast and in Eskimo-land this tool has its grip and its working part distinct. Finally, in the administration of the sinew for seizing, and the glue for binding all tight, one had only to watch the Apache Indian described in this text.

The arrows (*qaqdjung*) of the central Eskimos are made of round pieces of wood, generally tapering a little toward the lower end, to which two feathers of an owl or some other bird are attached. The bone heads of these arrows are joined to the shaft, as represented in Boas's fig. 443, p. 504. The difference in the methods used by the Mackenzie and the central tribes in fastening the point to the shaft is very striking. The arrow tang of the former and of the western tribes is pointed and inserted in the shaft (Boas's fig. 444, p. 505), while that of the latter is always beveled and lashed to it (Boas's figs. 442 and 443, p. 504). The direction of the bevel is either parallel or vertical to the edge (*id.* fig. 445, p. 505). Other forms of arrows are shown in *id.* fig. 446, p. 506. A similar difference between the fastenings of the foreshaft to the spear handle exists in the two localities. Western tribes give its base the form of a wedge (*id.* fig. 447, p. 506), which is inserted in the shaft, while the central Eskimos use a mortise. (Plates LII–LX.)

Formerly slate heads were in general use (*id.* fig. 448, p. 506); now the heads are almost everywhere made of iron or tin, riveted or tied to the

---

* *Eng. Scholar's Library.* Capt. J. Smith's works, No. 16, p. 68.

point (*id.* fig. 446, p. 506). In ancient graves flint heads are frequently found, some of which are represented in *id.* fig. 449, p. 507. On Southampton Island stone heads are in use even at the present time. Fig. 423, p. 491, probably shows how they were attached to the shank.*

The Panamint arrows are made from the stems of the reed (*Phragmites vulgaris*) and from willow shoots. The shafts are about 3½ feet long. Nearly mature, but still green, reeds are cut, their leaves removed, and the stems dried and straightened in the hands before a fire. Use is also made of a small stone, across the face of which have been cut two grooves large enough to admit an arrow shaft. This stone is heated, and a portion of the crude arrow is laid in one of the grooves until it is hot. The cane is then straightened by holding it crosswise in the teeth and drawing the end downward. By repeating this process throughout the whole length of the shaft a marvelously straight arrow is produced. The head of the arrow is a pin of very hard wood taken from some species of greasewood (*Striplex*). It is about 5 inches long, and tapers evenly to a blunt point. The base of the head is inserted about three-fourths of an inch into the hollow of the reed, and rests against the uppermost joint. It is bound in place by a thin band of sinew. At each joint of the arrow shaft is burned a ring of diagonal lines. The base of the shaft is notched to receive the bowstring, and feathered with three half feathers, bound on with sinews and twisted so as to give to the arrow a rotary motion.† (Pl. XLI, fig. 1.)

" The Spokane Indians laid a piece of buckskin on the hand, and from a flint pressed off flakes with a piece of deer's horn." These Indians belong to the Salishan family, and it is easy by means of the old material in the Museum to rehabilitate this ancient arrowmaker of Washington State. His process of flaking is that marked 4 in Plate I. The material on which he worked was incomparable, and his handiwork now forms the treasures of the Museum.

"At the base of Mount Uncle Sam" says Dulog, "on the west of Clear Lake, California, there is a tract 2 or 3 miles in extent covered with fragments of obsidian.

"With material so plentiful, the surrounding Indians are careful to choose only those pieces best shaped by nature for their purpose; but at places distant from the source of supply, the obsidian, which is often brought in large blocks, is chipped off in flakes from around a central core by blows of a rock.

"The old expert put on his left hand a piece of buckskin, with a hole cut in it to let the thumb pass through, something like the 'palm' used by sailmakers. This was of course to protect his hand while at work. In his right hand he took a tool of bone ground down to a blunt point. These tools, made often from the leg bone of a deer, are assorted in sizes, large ones being used for coarse work and small ones for fine work.

"A piece of obsidian of the right size was held in the left hand, then the right thumb was pressed on the top of the stone, while the point of

---

* Franz Boas. *The Central Eskimo*, VI *Rep. Bur. Ethnol.*, pp. 504–508.
† Coville, *Am. Anthrop.*, 1892, vol. V, p. 360.

the bone was strongly pressed against the under edge of the proposed arrowhead, and a little splinter of obsidian worked off. The operation was similar to the opening of a can with one of the old-fashioned can openers that work without leverage. Oftentimes material is spoiled in the sharpening. Around deserted camps piles of rejected fragments are sometimes found, either broken in putting on the edge or not being near enough the desired shape to pay for working up.

"A good deal of the sharpener's work, too, consisted in freshening up the edges of points blunted by use.

"One arrow-head, weather-worn by exposure, was shown me, with a border of fresh fractures extending from one-eighth to one-fourth of an inch in from the edge, where the sharpener's tool had been.

"There results from this process a serrated edge, which in the best specimens is beautifully fine and regular, but in rougher tools is often coarse. The old workman was careful of his stock in trade, and rolled up the fruit of his industry in a piece of ragged blanket to prevent its being injured while in transit from place to place."*

In this charming bit of description the old man played the following rôles:

(1) Discriminating the best pieces of stone to work, mineralogist.

(2) Obsidian knapper, stone-breaker.

(3) Flaker, with deer-horn tool working on the palm.

(4) As retouching injured blades, repairer of arrow-heads.

(5) Preserver of forms, a kind of wild Vishnu, laying up against future work all his stock in trade.

There seems to be little modern testimony to the assertion that the savage had learned to bevel the sides of his arrow heads alternately, for the purpose of making his arrow revolve in the air. Mr. Cushing has shown that this alternate beveling of the edges was a natural result of holding the piece of stone in a certain way along the thumb during the operation of chipping.

Lieut. Ray was the first to actually send to the National Museum a bit of antler, 6 inches long and about three-quarters of an inch in diameter, to be used like a stonecutter's punch or pitching tool or a smith's punch in knocking off chips in the process of arrow-making.† But there are constant references to this intermediary tool. The writer, who has experimented in most aborginal stone-working methods, has not attempted to use this apparatus in order to know its limits.

The substitution of hoop iron and other metal and glass for arrow-heads was one of the first lessons of acculturation learned by the American tribes. No custom or fashion was violated by this; the shaft and feather, that is, the manual part of the arrow, and all social and mythic portions remained unchanged.‡ This is the universal law of transfer from lower to higher grades. It is for the reason that woman's arts merely take better tools to do the very same work that savage women are easier to elevate than men.

---

* H. G. Dulog, in *Forest and Stream.*

† See *Smithsonian Report,* 1886.

‡ Cf. Timberlake, quoted by Jones, So. Indians, 251; Lawson, 252.

For straightening the shafts of arrows, and even the bone or ivory used for points, the aborigines employed a kind of wrench. In the south it was merely a convenient bit of wood, spindle-shaped, having a hole through the middle. The Utes used the end of the horn of the mountain sheep, perforated with holes of different sizes. The Plains Indians utilized the hard bones of the buffalo. The West Coast tribes made use of blocks of elk horn, and the Eskimo carved out of walrus ivory excellent tools for this purpose.* (Plate XXXIX.)

For grinding down and polishing arrow shafts the Indian had a special set of tools. There are in the U. S. National Museum from several localities small slabs of sandstone with a shallow groove running longitudinally in which the arrow shaft was laid and drawn back and forward. The leaves of grass containing siliceous matter served for the smoothing process. Finally, a smooth stone or bit of bone served to rub down the shaft and put on the finishing touches. The term "shaft grooves" is preferable for those straight or serpentine or zigzag furrows cut on an arrow shaft between the shaftment and the head or the foreshaft. They have been alleged to be symbolical of the lightning to invoke the spirit of destruction to dwell in the arrow. Others denominate them "blood-streaks," supposing they promote bleeding from a wound, so that the hunter could follow up his game by the trail of blood. The reed shafts never bear such streaks; the Eskimo do not make them, neither do the Northwest Coast Indians. Athapascan, Shoshonean, Siouan, Kaiowan tribes are especially given to this practice. The furrows do not always follow the same plan, and it would have been easy some years ago to work out series of patterns for these marks and determine their relation to tribes. They are in general: (1) straight and parallel; (2) wavy and sinuous; (3) zigzag, without design. (Pl. XLI, fig. 3.)

The same tribe used arrows of about one length and weight, as correct shooting, like good penmanship, is a balancing of a hundred sensibilities. Every good archer drew his bow to the arrow-head every shot, for near or for far. If one's bow be drawn always to arrow-head, and one's arrows be always of the same length, whether from his own quiver or from another's, the elements of variability are much reduced. It must be from some such cause that the arrows of each tribe agree so nearly in length. Indeed, since neighboring tribes shoot one another's arrows, there is undoubted inter-tribal agreement in length within limits. It is not here affirmed that the arrows of a tribe are exactly of a length. The variations are within certain narrow limits.

The author has measured a large number of quiver contents. The arrows of one quiver agree absolutely. The arrows of a tribe agree within a narrow margin. Often, especially in the buffalo region, there seemed to be a species of international agreement in the length of the arrow.

The foreshafted arrow finds its occasion first of all in the country of

---

* Boas., VI, *An. Rep. Bur. Ethnol.*, Washington, 525.

the reed cane—that is, along the southern portion of the United States. It may then be traced through those portions of California where the rhus, elder, and other pithy twigs abound. In the Eskimo area it has a multitude of structures and functions.

The foreshaft in the South and Southwest is a slender bit of hard wood sharpened and let into the top of the shaft and having the arrow-head attached to the fore end. The reasons are two. A hollow reed or a very pithy twig affords a very poor attachment for the arrow-head; and, secondly, this slenderer, heavier rod aids the directness of the flight. Indeed, the very long reed arrows of the Apache and Mohave tribes have for that reason insignificant feathers.

In the Eskimo arrows the heavy foreshaft of bone or ivory serves another purpose. Bone being heavier than wood, when one of these arrows is shot at an object in the water and the head is detached, the arrow stands perpendicular, and is dragged along by the divided line, the feather bobbing about and enabling the hunter to follow up his game.

In the harpoon arrow and the harpoon, the foreshaft furnishes an excellent socket piece for the barbed head or the "loose-shaft". There is no doubt, also, that its much greater specific gravity assists in the direct or straight-forward motion of the weapon. Many of these missiles are discharged into the water, in which case the ivory foreshaft is of great assistance.

It is often said by frontiersmen that the Plains Indians had two ways of mounting an arrow-head with relation to the notch at the nock. If the plane of the arrow-head be horizontal when the arrow is in position for shooting—that is, at right angles to the notch, the missile is a war arrow, to go between the ribs of men. But if the plane of the head be vertical when the bow is drawn, the missile is a hunting arrow for passing between the ribs of buffalo and other mammals.*

"Dodge explains that the Comanches place the notch of the arrow in the same plane with the notch of the string so that it may surely pass between the ribs of the animal which are up and down; for the same reason, the blade of the war arrow is perpendicular to the notch, the ribs of the human enemy being horizontal. (*Wild Indians*, San Francisco, 1882, 419.)

Captain Bourke thinks this is a mistake. He says, "I have seen all kinds in the same quiver."

There is more authority and reason for the assertion that the barbed arrowheads among these same Indians were for war and the leaf-shaped and rhomboidal heads were for hunting, because they could be easily withdrawn from the wound and used again; but the Eskimo have a barbed arrow, with ivory or bone barb piece, fitted into the head of the shaft in the most temporary fashion, so that when shot into an animal the head remains, rankles, and works its way into the flesh. For the

---

*On the plane of the head *cf*. Hansard, 212.

same reason the foreshafted arrows of the South and Southwest are loosely put together. The coloring of the shaft of arrows is technically called the riband. The Eastern tribes, the Basin tribes, and the Eskimo paint their arrows very little. Not much stress could be laid on this characteristic except on the California and Oregon coast. Here the author finds the following to be true: The arrows in the same quiver have the same riband. The arrows in the same tribe have the same general type of riband, and the same colors occur in old arrows. From tribe to tribe there occur differences in riband, but they have not been studied out.

The selling of prepared paints and dyes to the Indians by traders has introduced inextricable confusion into this characteristic. The riband on the arrow is generally in the shaftment or that portion of the arrow covered by the feathering. These bands and stripes have been called clan marks, owner marks, tribal marks, and the like, but they are not decisive in such matters.

According to Mr. Hough "African arrow-heads and feathering are fastened on with grass, palm-leaf strips, and other vegetable fibers, and many are tanged or socketed, and are not lashed at all."* Papuan arrows are served with vegetal fiber, the Ainos use bark, and in South America many tribes lash with natural fibers.

Most tribes of North America do not use any cement in fastening the head upon the shaft. The shrinking of the sinew is quite sufficient to hold all snugly in place. But in the Southwest of the United States, the *Algarobia glandulosa*, the *Prosopis juliflora*, and the *Laria mexicana* yield excellent gum, which is used by the Shoshonean and Yuman tribes to attach the arrow-head, without the use of the sinew.† (Pl. III, fig. 2.) Pine tree pitch and animal glue are also used.

The feathering of an arrow is an interesting study from place to place. It is governed by a host of considerations. As to this characteristic, arrows may be unfeathered, two feathered, three feathered, many feathered. The feathers vary in length from those only an inch to others a foot long; in adhesion, from those attached only at their extremities, and lying close or standing off, to others glued hard and fast to the shaftment their entire length. In some tribes the strips of feather are laid flat along the shaftment, as among the Eskimo and the west coast tribes, but in the great majority the feathers radiate from the shaft. In some tribes the strips of feathering are without ornament, in others they are shorn along the margins to be straight, triangular, and notched and a bit of downy feather is left at the nock as a streamer. In this respect, when carefully cut, some of the west-coast arrows present a decidedly natty appearance.

On one occasion an Apache Indian came to the author's department of the National Museum and, at his request, placed the feathering and

---

* *American Naturalist*, vol. IV, p. 61.   † *Am. Naturalist*, 1878, p. 595.

head upon an arrow. The feathers were split carefully and any excessive pith or horny portion of the quill removed. The pieces to form
the feathering were trimmed to the same length. The Indian next
shredded some sinew, which had been sent to the Museum from Hupa
Reservation in California, prepared by the relatives of the Apaches
that had been separated from them for centuries. This he chewed
until it was soft and pliant. He was now ready to lay on his feathers.
They were placed on the shaftment, wrapped slightly at the ends with
sinew to hold them in position until they could be adjusted to suit his
rigorous taste, at equal distances apart and at the proper distance
from the nock. Placing the shaft under his left arm and holding the
soft sinew in his right arm, he revolved the arrow with the thumb and
fingers of his left hand and guided the wrapping with his right hand.
Here was a primitive machine, with shaft and two bearings, used for
the purpose of winding evenly a thread upon a spool. The wrapping
or "seizing" of an Indian arrow is a very pretty and uniform piece of
work. Mr. Hough calls attention to the operation of this Apache fletcher
and gives drawing.* Among the northwestern Eskimos it is common
to neglect the seizing of sinew and to insert the ends of the quill portion
of the feather into the soft wood by means of a pointed ivory implement.
As mentioned, very many Eskimo arrows are found without feathers
at all, the very heavy foreshaft or iron head carrying the arrow forward
with sufficient accuracy. On the other hand, many of the barbed harpoons and bird tridents of the Eskimo are provided with feathers. In
the feathering of an arrow one feather must be uppermost, called in
archery the cock feather. In some beautiful specimens from Cooks
Inlet and near by one feather is snow white. But the author has
examined many hundreds of arrows without being able to detect that
the arrow-maker had in mind to draw attention to any one of the
feathers so as to create a true bottom and top to his missile. In the
Eskimo two-feathered arrow there is, of course, always one feather on
top and another under.

The number of feathers on a North American arrow is an exceedingly variable quantity. As a general rule the Eskimo have two and
the Indians three. This will do pretty well as a rule, but many three-
feathered and no-feathered arrows occur in Eskimo land, and among
Indain tribes no-feather arrows are common. The function of the
feather is to retard the rear end of the missile and cause the arrow to
go straight. This object being capable of accomplishment in other
ways the feather may be omitted.

The feathering of an arrow must be studied:

(1) The species of bird from which the feather is taken.
(2) The number of feathers, two, three, many.
(3) The shape and trimming of the feathers.

---

*American Anthropologist, IV, 61.

(4) Method of attachment, by siezing, or gluing, and to each of these there are many varieties.

(5) The part of the feather attached to the shaftment, close glued, standing off, or seized all along by a spiral sinew thread. In many museum specimens the glue has disap peared and feathers appear standing off that ought to be close laid.

The feathers of arrows are usually laid on in a line with the shaft, but many examples have come to light in which the feathers have a spiral direction on the shaftment. On one occasion the writer saw an Apache Indian finish the feathering of an arrow by seizing the two ends of the feathering and giving them a twist, simply to make the feathers lie flat on the arrow shaft. This goes for what it may be worth in accounting for the spiral position of many feathers. It is inconceivable that any savage should grasp the problem of the rifle bullet and construct his missile accordingly.

Captain J. G. Bourke, U. S. A., furnishes the following: "The Apaches use three hawk feathers, arranged equidistant along the shaft in the direction of the longer axis, fastened with sinew.

"The Uabes on the Amazon use three feathers spirally. (Wallace, *Amazon*, London, 1853, 493.)

"The Pimas of the Gila have two feathers instead of three. (*Cremony*, 103.)

"Mackenzie states that the Hare Indians of British North America who are, like the Apaches, members of the great Tinneh family, use but two feathers. (*Voyages*, London, 1800, 46.)

"According to Morgan, the arrows of the Iroquois had but two feathers and ended at the power extremity in a twist. (*League of the Iroquois*, N. Y., 1851, 306.)

"The arrows of the Apache-Yumas are feathered spirally with three feathers making a quarter-turn around the shaft. (Corbusier, in *Amer. Antiquarian*, November, 1886.)

"Maximilian, Prince of Wied, speaks of the feathers of the Mandan arrows being tied on at both ends like those of the Brazilians; he also speaks of the spiral line, either carved or painted red, which runs along the greater number of arrows, and says that it represents the lightning. (London, 1843, 389.)

"The explanation I received was that the runnel permitted the escape of blood and reduced the chances of expelling the arrow or the shaft."*

The nock of the American arrow is far more important than that on the bow. A good classification may be based on this characteristic as pointed out long ago by this writer. The following classes are easily recognized:

(1) The flat nock, as in all Eskimo arrows and in very few others.

(2) The cylindrical nock, most noteworthy on all reed arrow shafts of the South and in those of the far Orient.

(3) The bulbous nock, exaggerated in size on the West Coast, by cutting away the cedar wood as much as it would permit, and then wrap-

---

*J. G. Bourke, letter.

ping the butt end of the arrow with a narrow riband of birch bark until it resembled a small Turk's head knot. The Plains Indians also created a bulbous nock by whittling away the arrow shaft a fourth of an inch above the end, leaving a cylinder for a finger grip.

(4) The swallow-tail nock, an exceedingly dainty form affording a wide open notch and flaring finger grip, without waste of material. (Examples in Plates XLIII–XLVII.)

Notches for the bow-string were either very shallow, angular gashes, U-shaped cuts with parallel sides or gracefully curved incisions resembling the horizontal portion of the Greek letter psi.

Combining the notch with the nock the student has a mark which is helpful in deciding the band or tribe. At any rate, American arrows differ in both.

There is another characteristic noticeable at this point, the distance of the nock from the feathering. In some tribes the latter crowds down over the nock. In other, more dainty specimens, the feathering is several inches away.

This special characteristic connects itself with Prof. Morse's most interesting study respecting "arrow release." It will be easily seen that the thin, flat nock of the Eskimo lends itself easiest to the second or the third class of Prof. Morse, while the bulbous nock and the flaring nock conform most easily to his first class, in which the thumb and first joint of the forefinger pinch the butt of the arrow. Coming south, into the reed arrow country, where the nock is cylindrical, the Tertiary release might be looked for.

Dr. Shufeldt describes the method of arrow-release among the Navajoes.*

"Having read, with great interest, Prof. Morse's pamphlet on arrow-release, it was with no little curiosity that I handed a bow and two or three arrows to an old gray-headed warrior present, and asked him, 'Draw—as if you were about to kill the worst enemy you had in the whole world.' The old fellow seized the bow and arrows, and immediately drew one of them to its very head. This is the position he stood in at the time: His left foot was slightly in advance of the right, the bow was firmly seized at its middle with the left hand, while it was held somewhat obliquely, the upper moiety inclining toward the right from the vertical line, and, of course, the lower limb having a corresponding inclination toward the left side. The two spare arrows were held with the bow in the left hand, being confined by the fingers against its right outer aspect. With the right hand he seized the proximal end of the arrow in the string, using the thumb and index finger, at a point fully an inch or more above the notch, and consequently including the feathers. The ring finger bore against the string below this seizure, and its pressure was re-enforced by its being overlapped by the middle digit, the little finger being curled within the palm of the hand.

"This corresponded to Prof. Morse's secondary release as figured on page 8, of the above referred-to pamphlet, with the exception that the middle finger should overlap the annularis, and was not of itself used

---

* *Am. Nat.*, vol. XXI, p. 784.

to draw back the string. I noticed, too, that the arrow at its head was on the *left side* of the bow and simply rested on top of his clinched hand. This man wore, in common with all the others who used the bow, a stiff leather bracer, fastened by buckskin strings about his left wrist, the collar being about 2 inches deep, and this, in several others who stood near and who wore them, was ornamented with silver buttons. He drew the arrow back and forth three or four times without changing the position of his finger or hands, when I suddenly asked him to shoot as if he were going to kill a squirrel running up a tree. He smiled at this and simply drew the bow the *same way.* Upon further questioning him, he told me that the Navajoes rarely held their spare arrows in the bow hand, as he now had them, but carried a scabbard (quiver of buckskin) full, in front of them, from which they could be removed with great rapidity while firing; this he immediately demonstrated to me from one of the scabbards worn by an Indian there present."

In archery-arrows and in Asiatic examples a piece of hard wood is inserted at the nocking end of the arrow. But in American arrows the nock is always a part of the wood of the shaft. This piece, in technical language, is called the "footing," but it need not be here discussed.

The subject of poisoned arrows in North America is a vexed one. A very high authority has said that the thing was unknown. But I have the testimony of Bourke to the contrary. No one avers that these aborigines prepared a vegetable poison, like the curari. But the toxic effect of putrid flesh was known, whether or not bitten freely by rattlesnakes. Dr. W. J. Hoffman will bring together the evidence on this subject.[*]

Powiaken, a Salish chief, declared to Mrs. McBean that obsidian and glass points in arrows were poisonous (U. S. N. M. letter).

The Koniagas poisoned their arrow and lance points with a preparation of aconite, by drying and pulverizing the root, mixing the powder with water and, when it fermented, applying it to their weapons.

Bourke furnishes the following: "Selecting the roots of such plants as grow alone, these are dried and pounded or grated." (*Sauer, Billing's Ex., 178.*)

They made arrow points of copper, obtaining a supply from the Kenai of Copper River; and the wood was as finely finished as if turned in a lathe.

"Die Pfeilspitzen sind aus Eisen oder Kupfer ersteres erhalten sie von den Kenayern, letzteres von den Tutnen." (*Baer, Stat. u. Ethn., 118.*)

"De pedernal en forma de arpon, cortado contanta delicadeza como pudiera hacerlo el mas habil lapidario." (*Bodega y Quadra, Nav., MS., 66.*)[†]

---

[*] For Southern Indians, see Jones, p. 248.   [†] See Bancroft, Native Races, I., 79.

THE QUIVER.

The quiver is difficult to study, because collectors have paid little attention to it. Among all the Plains tribes they are objects of beauty, and have been gathered as bric-a-brac, with little information of their whereabouts. (Pl. LXXVII–XCIV.) The same rules are to be observed in the study of the quiver that we apply to all other objects connected with aboriginal industries. The quiver is largely of the region. In the first place the material out of which each example is made must be furnished by nature; hence it is of sealskin in one place, of cedar wood in another, of soft pelt in another, and in the south land is frequently made of some kind of soft basketry. Again, the structure of the quiver must be adapted to its function, that is, to the bow and arrows to be carried; also to the exigencies of the weather and the surroundings. The parts of a most elaborate quiver are:

(1) The bow case, a long, slender bag, into which the bow is thrust.

(2) The arrow case, a pocket in which the arrows are kept, points downward, as a rule.

(3) The stiffener, a rod of wood attached along the outside of the arrow case, to keep it rigid.

(4) Baldric, a band of buckskin, or in the finest examples, of elegant fur, lined and decorated with quill work, passing over the left shoulder, across the breast, and attached by its ends to the quiver. It is for carrying the quiver.

(5) Fire bag, a leather pouch in which the Indian hunter kept his flints, steel, spunk, awl, and other subsidiary apparatus needful on his journey. It was tied to the middle of the bow case or the stiffener. Among several of the mountain tribes the squaw lavished all her skill upon her husband's quiver. The costliest beaver, marten, otter, and mountain lion pelt was invoked. It was lined with soft buckskin, or in later times with red strouding. Beads of every imaginable color were worked upon the border of the arrow case and upon the lining of the long pendant therefrom. Strips of fur, daintily cut in fringes, were sewed about the bottom of the bow case, and every spot capable of rich decoration received it. Between this and the plain salmon-skin capsule, into which the Eskimo thrust his arrows, there are many gradations of quivers, as will appear in the treatment of the several tribes.

"The quiver of the Central Eskimo, says Boas, is made of seal-skin, the hair of which is removed. It comprises three divisions, a larger one containing the bow and a smaller one containing 4 or 6 arrows, the head directed toward the lower end of the case. When extracted from the quiver they are ready for use. Between the two compartments there is also a small pouch, in which tools and extra arrow-heads are carried. (Plate XCIII).

"When travelling the Eskimo carry the quiver by an ivory handle; when in use it is hung over the left shoulder. Boas's fig. 451, p. 508, represents quiver handles, the first being fashioned in imitation of an ermine." *

---

* F. Boas, *The Central Eskimo*, VI *Rep. Bur. Ethnol.*, p. 508.

"The quiver of the Blackfeet was made from the cougar skin and was frequently valued at one horse."*

Throughout the area of fur-bearing animals the pelt of any one of them of sufficient size served as a quiver or arrow bag. These are, for the most part, slovenly in appearance. But the Blackfeet and other Plains tribes formerly made up their bow cases and quivers from large skins. In later times leather and cow's hide with the hair on were substituted. The elaborate make-up was preserved.

"The Yurok quiver was made of the skin of the raccoon or marten turned wrongside out and suspended by a string. In the lower end moss was stuffed as a cushion for the arrow-heads.† The bow was stuffed into this bag with the arrows and the wonder is how a man could keep the bow from destroying the arrows. In traveling, however, the bow was held in the left hand.

NOTES ON THE BOWS, ARROWS, AND QUIVERS OF VARIOUS TRIBES.

Baegert says that the shafts of the Southern California arrows consist of reeds, which they straighten by the fire. They are above 6 spans long, and have, at the lower end, a notch to catch the string, and 3 or 4 feathers about a finger long, not much projecting, and let into slits made for that purpose. At the upper end of the shaft a pointed piece of heavy wood, a span and a half long, is inserted, bearing usually at its extremity a flint of a triangular shape, almost resembling a serpent's tongue and indented like the edge of a saw. The Californians carry their bows and arrows always with them, and as they commence at an early age to use these weapons many of them become skillful archers.‡ (Plate XCI, XCII.)

The arms of the Apaches according to Pike are the bow and arrow. Their bow forms two demicircles, with a shoulder in the middle; the back of it is entirely covered with sinews, which are laid on in so nice a manner by the use of some glutinous substance as to be almost imperceptible; this gives great elasticity to the weapon. Their arrow is more than the "cloth yard" of the English, being $3\frac{1}{4}$ feet long, the upper part consisting of some light rush or cane, into which is inserted a shaft of about 1 foot made of some hard, seasoned light wood; the point is of iron, bone, or stone, and when the arrow enters the body, in attempting to extract it the shaft [foreshaft] comes out of its socket and the point remains in the wound. With this weapon they shoot with such force as to go through the body of a man at a distance of 100 yards.§

"The Apache arrow was composed of three distinct parts—the reed, the stem, and the barb; the last affixed to the stem, and the stem, of

---

* *Maximilian, Travels, etc.,* 257.

† Powers, *Cont. to N. A. Ethnol.,* vol. III, p. 48.

‡ Baegert, Jacob, *Aboriginal Inhabitants of Californian Peninsula, Sm. Rep.,* 1863, p. 362.

§ *Pike's Expedition,* Phila., 1810, 10, Appendix to Part III.

hard wood, inserted in the reed, and both held firmly in place by ligatures of sinew. The stem was made of a hard wood called kk-ing, and the reed in Apache 'klo-ka,' meaning 'arrow grass.' There is a great advantage in the use of this reed, because the arrow afterwards needs no straightening, whereas the arrows made by the Zuñis and others must be subjected to a special process to make them shoot true.

"The use of sinew for securing the barb to the stem was believed to be based upon the fact that after the arrow had entered the body the warm blood, flowing from the wound, would soften and loosen the sinew, disengage the barb, and increase the discomfort, pain, and danger to the victim.

"It may be of interest to students of linguistics to know that the Apache word for bullet, 'ka,' is really the word for arrow, and much as the word has survived the weapon itself has survived, because the cross section of a rifle bullet, taken along the greater axis, is all the same as the same section made on a double-tanged arrow."*

"In the *American Naturalist*, vol. XL, p. 264, Mr. Edwin A. Barber describes nine different kinds of arrow-heads—leaf-shaped, triangular, indented at base, stemmed, barbed, beveled, diamond-shaped, awl-shaped, shaped like a serpent's head.

"All the above forms may be found in use among the Apaches to-day. The same warrior may have in his quiver representatives of several types, sometimes serrated, sometimes non-serrated, but all deadly. Arrows intended simply for the killing of birds or small game were not always barbed, but were generally provided with a cross piece about 2 inches below the tip. [This same stop is found in Canada.]

"The arrow of the Apache sometimes terminates in a triangular piece of hard wood, which seems to be perfectly effective as a weapon. One set of these is now in my possession, made of Florida orange wood by Koth li, a Chiricahua prisoner confined at Fort Marion.

"Just such arrows were observed by Columbus upon first reaching this continent. 'They carry however in lieu of arms, canes dried in the sun, on the ends of which they fix heads of wood, dried and sharpened to a point.' (Letters of Columbus, Hakluyt Soc., London, 1847, vol. II, p. 6.) *

"Stone arrow-heads were made preferably of obsidian (dolguini), next of chalcedony, petrified wood, jasper, or other siliceous rock, lastly of fragments of beer bottles; but if pieces of hoop iron could be picked up they were always utilized.

"Arrows made out of domestic glass were described over a century ago by Lawson, in his account of the Carolina Indians. He mentions having seen in an Indian town, 'very long arrows headed with pieces of glass which they had broken from bottles.' (Quoted by Squier and Davis, Mounds of the Mississippi Valley, in *Smithsonian Contributions*, vol. VI, 213; but there the opinion is expressed that these may have been obsidian.)

"It may be well to remember that the Indians of the Southwest were perfectly familiar with obsidian, and that the Apache name for glass means obsidian. It may have been only a coincidence, but I do not at this moment remember any glass arrows that were not brown glass, the nearest approach in appearance to obsidian. I have seen the green arrows, but they were made of the semi-precious stone called *aqua marina*, found among the Navajoes.

"Lyon, quoted by Bancroft (*Nat. Races*, vol. I, p. 342), refers to an

---

* J. G. Bourke, letter.

Indian (tribe not given) who made him a glass arrow from a fragment of porter bottle at the third trial, after he had learned the grain of the glass.

"The process of manufacture was in each case the same, and consisted in chipping small fragments from the edges of suitable pieces of material, the chipping implement being a portion of hardened deer or elk horn held in the right hand, the siliceous stone being held in the left over a flap of buckskin to protect the fingers.

"I once made it my business to solve the problem how long it would take Apaches whose village had been captured and destroyed by troops to provide themselves anew with weapons which would render them a menace to the scattered settlements of the frontier. I singled out an Apache at random and stipulated that he should employ no tools of iron, but allowed him to gather from the ground such chips of chalcedony as he pleased.

"He made a number of barbs, the time as recorded in my note-books being five, six, seven, and eight minutes; an expert might have done even better than that.

"I can not understand what Powers meant when he said that a Pomo Indian will spend days and even weeks upon one piece, unless he is alluding to some one making a 'medicine bow and arrows for a special occasion'. (Bancroft, *Nat. Races*, vol. I, p. 342.)

"Gen. George Crook, who was a very close observer of the habits and customs of the wild tribes among whom he served, relates that the Indians of Oregon used obsidian and made the barbs with remarkable facility and rapidity, from fifty to sixty in an hour. (*Smithsonian Report*, 1871.) He also states that the Klamaths were making their arrows of broken junk bottles, the tool used, a knife in place of a horn, and a blanket instead of a buckskin.

[Captain Bourke is evidently thinking of the making of arrow heads. Every tribe of Indians spent days and even weeks upon arrow shafts and bows. As in the manufacture of pottery the operation can not be finished at a single sitting as has been shown previously.]

"The Hoopa Indian, who is a relative of the Apache, makes his arrows in much the same manner, but the obsidian or jasper head is untanged and lashed with sinew."*

"Catlin says that every Apache tribe has its factory in which arrow-heads are made, and in those only certain adepts are allowed to make them for the use of the tribe. Erratic bowlders of flint are collected (and sometimes brought an immense distance) and broken with a sort of sledge-hammer, made of a rounded pebble of hornstone, set in a twisted withe, holding the stone and forming a handle.

"The stone, at the indiscriminate blows of the sledge, is broken into a hundred pieces, and such flakes selected as, from the angles of their fracture and thickness, will answer as the basis of an arrow-head; and in the hands of the artisan they are shaped into the beautiful forms and proportions which they desire, and which are to be seen in most of our museums.

"The master workman, seated on the ground, lays one of these flakes on the palm of his left hand, holding it firmly down with two or more fingers of the same hand, and with his right hand, between the thumb and two forefingers, places his chisel (or punch) on the point that is to be broken off; and a co-operator (a striker) sitting in front of him, with

---

*Capt. J. G. Bourke, letter.

a mallet of very hard wood, strikes the chisel (or punch) on the upper end, flaking the flint off on the under side, below each projecting point that is struck. The flint is then turned and chipped in the same manner from the opposite side, and so turned and chipped until the required shape and dimensions are obtained, all the fractures being made on the palm of the hand.

"In selecting a flake for the arrow-head a nice judgment must be used or the attempt will fail; a flake with two opposite parallel or nearly parallel planes is found, and of the thickness required for the center of the arrow-point. The first chipping reaches near to the center of these planes, but without quite breaking it away, and each chipping is shorter and shorter, until the shape and the edge of the arrow-head are formed.

"The yielding elasticity of the palm of the hand enables the chip to come off without breaking the body of the flint, which would be the case if they were broken on a hard substance. These people have no metallic instruments to work with, and the instrument (punch) which they use I was told was a piece of bone; but on examining it I found it to be a substance much harder, made of the tooth (incisor) of the sperm whale, or sea lion, which are often stranded on the coast of the Pacific. This punch is about 6 or 7 inches in length and 1 inch in diameter, with one rounded side and two plane sides; therefore presenting one acute and two obtuse angles to suit the points to be broken.

"This operation is very curious, both the holder and the striker singing, and the strokes of the mallet given exactly in time with the music, and with a sharp and rebounding blow, in which, the Indians tell us, is the great medicine (or mystery of the operation).

"The bows also of this tribe, as well as the arrow-heads, are made with great skill, either of wood and covered on the back with sinew, or of bone, said to be brought from the sea-coast, and probably from the sperm whale. These weapons, much like those of the Sioux and Comanches, for use on horseback, are short, for convenience of handling, and of great power, generally of 2½ feet in length, and their mode of using them in war and the chase is not surpassed by any Indians on the continent."*

"The bows of the Beothucs are all of sycamore, which being very scarce in their country, and the only wood it produces that is fit for this use, becomes very valuable. Mr. Peyton informed Lloyd that their bows were roughly made of mountain ash or dogwood; they were formed by splitting the piece of wood selected for the purpose down the middle, the round side of which formed the back of the bow. The sticks are not chosen with any nicety, some of them being knotty and very rude in appearance, but they show a considerable amount of constructive skill. Except in the grasp the inside of them is cut flat, but so obliquely and with so much skill that the string will vibrate in a direction coinciding directly with the thicker edge of the bow. The bow is fully 5½ feet long. The string was made of deer's sinew.

"Beothuc arrows were made of pine (white) or sycamore, and were slender, light, and straight. The head was a two-edged lance about 6 inches long, made of iron taken from the traps, and other objects of that metal, which they had stolen from the furriers and fishermen.

"Cartwright says, in his journal of a residence in Labrador, that the head of the arrow was a barbed lance 6 inches long made out of an old

---

* George Catlin, *Last Rambles*, pp. 187 to 190, in *Smithsonian Report*, 1885, p. 743.

nail let into a cleft in the top of the shaft, and secured there by a thread of deer's sinew. The stock was about 3 feet in length. It was feathered with the 'gray goose wing.' They also use the feathers of the 'gripp,' or sea eagle, on their arrows."*

This testimony is of the same character as that relating to John Smith. The Beothucs did not belong to any of the great Indian families known, but were a stock apart. The rudeness of manufacture is also noticeable in contrast with those of the Eskimo.

"The weapons used in the Ioway tribe, and of which these people have brought many, are very similar to those used in most of the uncivilized tribes of North America, consisting of the bow and arrows, the lance and the javelin, war-clubs, knives, etc., and with these, as a protection in battle, a leathern shield, made of the hide of the buffalo bull, sufficiently thick and hard to arrest an arrow or to turn the blade of a lance."†

The Ioways belong to the Siouan stock and their arrows are a shaft, iron head, and three tolerably long feathers. The nock is either bulbous or flaring, affording a grip for the thumb and fore finger. The quiver is an elaborate affair. Indeed the quivers of the Siouan and other stocks preying upon the buffalo were the most complicated on the continent.

The Blackfeet do not make bows of the horn of the elk or of the mountain sheep. Their country does not produce any wood suitable for bows, and they obtain by barter the bow wood, or yellow wood (*Maclura aurantiaca*) from the river Arkansas. For their quivers they prefer the skin of the cougar (*Felis concolor*, Linn). The tail hangs down from the quiver, is trimmed with red cloth on the inner side, embroidered with white beads and ornamented at the end or elsewhere with strips of skin-like tassels.

"I saw few lances among the Blackfeet, but many war clubs which they have taken from the Flatheads. Many have thick leather shields painted green and red, and hung with feathers and other things."‡

All the Sioux tribes use a short arrow, with long shaftment bearing three eagle feathers. The shafts were marked with the lightning furrows, and streaked in different colors. The Sioux procured iron centuries ago and substituted it for the stone head. One of the rarest specimens in any museum is a Sioux arrow with a jasper point.

Mr. Dorsey says that the Omaha use the following as their arrow-measures: From the inner angle of the elbow to the tip of the middle finger, and thence over the back of the hand to the wrist bone.

"When in need of arrow points the Sioux would take his rawhide or buckskin sack or bag and go in search of the above-mentioned stones; when found would take another heavy stone, and by striking and breaking the stone, would gather the fragments that would serve for arrow or spear points. Those flakes which required less work in trimming or

---

* T. G. B. Lloyd, *J. Anthrop. Inst.*, vol. IV, p. 28.
† Catlin's Indian Gallery, *Smithsonian Report*, 1885, part II, p. 148.
‡ Consult Maximilian, *Trav.*, 1843, p. 258.

chipping would be placed in his sack, and when enough were collected he would take them to his lodge to fashion. Holding the arrow, spear, or knife piece in his hand, he would chip carefully with another flint or iron rock, or placing the sharp edge against the projecting piece or particle to be removed, being careful in only chipping or forcing off sufficient to make the stone in proper shape, with sharp edge and point. They made the grooves in war clubs, axes, hammers, or bone breakers by constant pecking.

"There was another kind of arrow point they made of which I never heard before, and that was out of the front part of the foreleg of an elk, between fetlock and knee joint. They would take that bone and break it, and slivers that would answer were made into arrow points by grinding them on a stone. They make a good arrow point, but not so strong as the flint points.

"The stone arrow points were each separately bound with sinews to protect them from breaking even in the quiver, and the arrows were unwrapped before starting after a herd of buffalo."*

The unwrapping of the sinew before shooting is quite new testimony, but Mr. Allen has lived on the frontier many years in Montana.

"Among the plains Indians," says Dodge "a good bow takes a long time and much labor in its construction. The best wood is the osage orange ('*bois d'arc*' of the old French trappers, corrupted into 'bow dark' by plains Americans). This wood grows in comparatively a limited area of country, and long journeys are sometimes made to obtain it. Only the best are selected, straight, and as free as possible from knots. The seasoning process is slow and very thorough. A little cutting, shaping, and scraping with knife or piece of glass, then a hard rubbing with buffalo fat or brains, and the stick is put aside in a warm place, to be worked at again in a few days or weeks. A good bow with fair usage will last many years, but it is liable to be broken at any time by accident. Each warrior, therefore, possesses several sticks of bow wood in various stages of completion.

"The strings are formed of closely-twisted fibers of the sinews of animals. These sinews are cut out their full length. Each is then subdivided longitudinally into strings, and these picked and re-picked into fibers as fine as hair and as long as possible. With the rude means at their disposal it requires no little skill so to put and twist these fibers together as to form a string perfectly round and of precisely the same size and tension from end to end.

"The arrows require in the aggregate much more labor than the bow. Any hard, tough, straight-grained wood is used. It is scraped to proper size and shape, and must be perfectly round. The head is either of stone or iron—of late years almost exclusively of iron, for stone of the necessary hardness is extremely difficult to work, and twenty or more stones are spoiled or broken for each arrow-head made.

"Under the most favorable circumstances, however, the most skillful Indian workman can not hope to complete more than a single arrow in a hard day's work. In a short fight, or an exciting dash after game, he will expend as many arrows as will keep him busily at work for a month to replace.†

"The constructive industry of the men was confined principally to the making of arms, bows, arrows, shields, and spears. These were all objects in which they took great pride. The favorite material for bows

---

* Letter from I. Allen, Stillwater, Mont.

† Dodge, *Plains of the Great West*, Putnam, 1877, pp. 348, 349.

was *bois d'arc* (*Maclura aurantiaca*). When these could not be obtained hickory or coffee bean (*Gymnocladus Canadensis*) was used. The name *ti-rak-is*, bow, seem to indicate that bows were once made of bone, the ribs of the buffalo or other large animal, skillfully fitted and wrapped throughout with sinew. Forty years ago bows of this kind, and also of elk horn were occasionally found in use. Choice bows were sometimes made of red cedar, and if carefully used answered well, but were extremely liable to be shattered by any rough handling. The making of a good bow was a task involving long and painstaking labor. It was wrought into shape only a little at a time, being repeatedly oiled meanwhile, and constantly handled to keep the wood-pliable. When finished the bow was sometimes wrapped with sinew and its strength thereby greatly increased. The string was of sinew from the back of the buffalo. As soon as the sinew was taken from the animal the particles of flesh adhering were scraped off and the minute fibres carefully separated. The best of these were selected and twisted into a string of uniform size and elasticity. One end of this string was fastened securely in place upon the bow, and the other furnished with a loop so adjusted that in an instant, as occasion required, the bow might be strung or unstrung.

"According to Dunbar much labor was spent by the Pawnees in the construction of arrows. The shafts were made from sprouts of dogwood (*Cornus stolonifera*). The bark was removed and the rods were rubbed between two grooved stones, held firmly together in one hand till reduced to a proper size and smoothness. The head, made of hoop iron, was then inserted in one end of the shaft and bound in position with sinew. The back end of the shaft was now furnished with a triple row of feathers attached by means of glue and sinew and the end notched to fit the bowspring. With a small chisel-like instrument three slight grooves or channels were cut along the shaft between the head and the feathers and the arrow was complete. Various reasons were assigned for this channeling. Some claimed that it caused the arrow to adhere more firmly in the wound; others that it was simply designed to facilitate the flow of blood. The manufacture of arrows, as of bows, was a slow and irksome process. Three or four were probably the limit of a day's work, even after the rough material was already at hand. So exact were they in making them that not only were the arrows of different tribes readily distinguishable, but even individuals could recognize their own arrows when thrown together with those of others of the same band. Disputes sometimes arose after the slaughter of a herd of buffalo as to whose some particular carcass rightfully was. If the arrow still remained in the body the question was easily decided by drawing it out and examining the make of it. Some Indians made two kinds of arrows, one for hunting and another for war. In the latter the head was so fastened that when an attempt was made to draw the shaft from a wound the head was detached and remained in the body of the victim. The Pawnee never used such. When once he had possessed himself of a good bow and a supply of arrows the Pawnee was as solicitous in the care of them as a hunter would be of a choice rifle. The bow, if not in actual service, was kept close in its case, and the arrows in the quiver. Great pains were taken that they should not become by any chance wet, and much time was spent handling them, that the bow should not lose its spring and the arrows should not warp. The average length of the former was 4 feet; of the latter 26 inches."*

---

* J. B. Dunbar: *Pawnee Indians*, sec. 20.

The case for the bow and the quiver are of the skin of some animal, often of otter, fastened to each other; and to the latter the tail of the animal at full length is appended. The bow is partly covered with elk horn, has a very strong string of twisted sinews of animals, and is wound round in different places with the same to strengthen it. The bow is often adorned with colored cloth, porcupine quills and white strips of ermine.*

"The Pawnee bow case and quiver were made of skin, dressed to be impervious to moisture. The usual material was elk skin. Indians who could afford it sometimes made a quiver and case of the skin of an otter or panther. In removing a skin which was to be used for this purpose from the carcass, care was exercised that every particle of the skin, that of the head, tail, and even the claws, should be retained, and appear in the case when finally made up. Cases of this make, with their heavy coating of fur virtually waterproof, were very highly prized."†

"The bow-makers of both the Hupa and Klamath tribes," says Ray, "are specialists, and the trade is now confined to a very few old men. I have here seen no man under 40 years of age that could make a bow or an arrow, and only one old man who could make a stone arrow-head.

"To make a bow, the wood of a yew sapling 2½ to 3 inches in diameter is selected and rough-hewn to shape, the heart side inward and the back carefully smoothed to the form of the back of the bow. The sinew is laid on while the wood is green and held in place until dry by means of a twine wrapping. In this condition it is hung in the sweat house until the wood is thoroughly seasoned, when it is finished and strung, and in some cases the back is varnished and painted. The most delicate part of the operation is to get the proper tension on the sinew backing. If too tight the wood crimps or splinters when the bow is strung, and a lack of proper tension leaves the bow weak and worthless. When the bow is seasoned it has a reverse curve of about 3 inches.

"The sinew for the backing and bow-string is taken from the back and the hind leg of the deer at the time of killing, and dried for future use. When required it is soaked until pliable, stripped into fine shreds and laid on by commencing at each end and terminating at the center of the bow. The sinew is slightly twisted and dried before it is placed on the bow.

"The glue used to fix the backing is obtained by boiling the gland of the lower jaw and the nose of the sturgeon. This is dried in balls and preserved for use, and is prepared by simply dipping it in warm water and rubbing it on the wood.

"The arrow shafts are usually made from the wood of the wild currant, and are worked to shape with a knife and tried by the eye. After roughing they are allowed to season and are then finished. Any curves are taken out with a straightener, made of a piece of hard wood, spindle shaped and perforated in the middle. The arrow-heads used in war and for big game are usually made from flint and obsidian, and more recently of iron and steel. The flakes for the stone heads are knocked off by means of a pitching tool of a deer antler. The stone heads are made with a chipper composed of a crooked handle, to which is lashed

---

*Maximilian, *Travels*, London, 1843, p. 195, mentions that the Sioux bows are similar.

†J. B. Dunbar: *The Pawnee Indians*.

a short piece of antler precisely similar to those which I collected at Point Barrow. The work is held in the left hand on a pad and flaked off by pressure with a tool in the right hand in exactly the same manner as I found the Innuits doing in northern Alaska.

"The bows made by these people are effective for game up to 50 or 75 yards, and would inflict a serious wound at 100 yards. At 50 yards the arrows will penetrate a deer from 5 to 10 inches. I never heard of one passing entirely through a deer.*

"Eells says that "bows and arrows are used at present by the Twana in Washington state only as playthings, and are very poor; but formerly they were very common. The bows were about 3 feet long, and were made of yew wood, the strings of sinews or the intestines of raccoons. The arrows were about 2½ feet long, were made of cedar, with feathered shafts, and points of stone, and of nails, after they obtained them; and the quiver of wolf skin. Arrow-heads are sometimes made of brass or iron, 2 or 3 inches long, half an inch wide, and very thin, and also of very hard wood, 5 inches long, and round. Sometimes, for birds, they are made of iron-wood, about 5 inches long, with two prongs, one of them being half an inch shorter than the other."†

According to Capt. Wilkes the Klamet bows and arrows are made the first of yew about 3 feet long, flat, 1½ to 2 inches wide, backed with sinew and painted. The arrows are over 30 inches long, some of close-grained wood, a species of Spiraca, others of reed. Feathers are 5 to 8 inches long. The barbed head of obsidian is inserted in a fore shaft 3 to 5 inches long. This is left in the wound. Shallow blood channels are sometimes cut in the shaft. The bow is held horizontally, braced by the thumb of the left hand and drawn by the thumb and three fingers of right hand. The chest is thrown back and the right leg forward in shooting. Quivers are of deer, raccoon, or wild-cat skins.‡

The Clallam bows were short and small, made of yew. The arrows were small and pointed with bone or iron.§ The Clallams are one of the Salishan tribes from whom Wilkes gathered many bows and arrows, now in the National Museum. The arrow shafts are of cedar, and have a large, bulbous nock, wrapped with birch bark. Some of them have two-barbed points of wood, bone, or metal.

Bows of the Shushwap were formerly made chiefly of wood of the juniper (*Juniperus occidentalis*), named poontlp. They were also sometimes made of yew (*Taxus brevifolia*), named skin-ik, though this tree is scarcely to be found in the Shushwap country. It is reported however to grow far up in the North Thompson Valley. The bow was often covered on its outer surface with the skin of a rattlesnake, which was glued on in the same manner which was customary among some of the tribes of the Great Plains. Arrows were made of the wood of the service berry. Arrow-heads and spear-heads were made of various kinds of stone, always chipped.||

---

* P. H. Ray.

† Rev. M. Eells, Hayden's *Bull.*, 1877, 3, pp. 78–79.

‡ Cf. Wilkes, *Narrative*, vol. v., p. 239.

§ Wilkes, *Narrative*, IV, 299.

|| "People of British Columbia." G. M. Dawson, p. 17.

"The native bow in Vancouver's island is beautifully formed. It is generally made of yew or crab-apple wood, and is 3½ feet long, with about 2 inches at each end turned sharply backward from the string. The string is a piece of dried seal gut, deer sinew, or twisted bark. The arrows about 20 inches long, and are made of pine or cedar, tipped with 6 inches of serrated bone, or with two unbarred bone or iron prongs. I have never seen an Aht arrow with a barbed head." (Sproat's *Scenes*, p. 82.)

"Having now, to a great extent, discarded the use of the traditional tomahawk and spear. Many of these weapons are, however, still preserved as heirlooms among them." (Barrett-Lennards Trav., p. 42.)

"No bows and arrows. Generally fight hand to hand, and not with missiles." (Fitzwilliam's Evidence, *in Hudson Bay Co., Rept.*, 1857, 115.)*

"The arrows and spears in Puget Sound were usually pointed with bone; the bows were of yew, and though short, were of great power. Vancouver describes a superior bow used at Puget Sound. It was from 2½ to 3 feet long, made from a naturally curved piece of yew, whose concave side became the convex of the bow, and to the whole length of this side a strip of elastic hide or serpent skin was attached so firmly by a kind of cement as to become almost a part of the wood. This lining added greatly to the strength of the bow, and was not affected by moisture. The bowstring was made of sinew." Vancouver's *Voy.*, vol. I, p. 253.

"At Gray Harbor the bows were somewhat more circular than elsewhere." (Vancouver's *Voy.*, vol. II, p. 84; Wilkes's *Nar. in U. S. Exploring Expedition*, pp. 14, 319; Kane's *Wand.*, pp. 209, 210.)†

Lieut. Allen, U. S. Army, has described the excessive pains which the Copper River Indians bestow upon the fashioning and caring for their bows. There are no first rate, tough, elastic woods near them. Birch and willow and such soft species are the only stock in trade. And yet, by dint of heating or toasting, boiling, greasing, and rubbing down they convert these poor materials into excellent arms. It is here that the wooded wrist guard or bridge is attached to the grip on the inside.

The Hong Kutchin Indians (Athapascan family) closely allied with Lieut. Allen's people, make their bows of willow after the same painstaking fashion, and their arrows of pine. The bows are almost straight, and in order to prevent the string from lacerating the wrist they do not wear a wrist guard, but lash a bit of wood to the inside of the grip (*see* Plate II). The Kutchin tribes all use a similar bow, but do without the guard. The quiver is simply a bag of skin worn under the left arm. It has two loops for the bow and the arrows are inserted notch down.‡

"The arrow-heads of the Kutchin are of bone for wild fowl, or bone tipped with iron for moose or deer; the bow is about 5 feet long, and that of the Hong-Kutchin is furnished with a small piece of wood 3 inches long by 1½ broad, and nearly 2 thick, which projects close to the part grasped by the hand. This piece catches the string and prevents it from striking the hand, for the bow is not bent much. There are no individuals whose trade is to make spears, bows, or arrows."

---

* See Bancroft, Native Races, vol. I, p. 188.
† *id*. 214–215.
‡ Jones, *Smithsonian Report*, 1866, pp. 322, 324.

"The Kutchin still retain the bow, which is of the same shape through all the tribes, with the exception of the small guard in the Hong-Kutchin bow, mentioned before. The quiver is the same, and worn under the left arm; it is furnished with two small loops to hold the bow, thus leaving the hunter both hands free to use his gun. The arrows are placed in the quiver with the notch downwards. The Kut-chin are not expert with the bow; no doubt they were better shots before firearms were introduced among them. The bow is made of willow and will not send an arrow with sufficient force to kill a deer more than from 50 to 60 yards. The arrows are made of pine."*

Father Morice says that "the only pursuit for which our Dene may be said to have been amply provided with home-made implements was war and its allied occupation, hunting. The offensive weapons in use among them were arrows, spears, lances, and *casse-tetes.*

"The only really polished stone implement of Dene manufacture was the *eaelh* or *casse tete.* The specimen illustrated is of a hard gran-ite stone. A variety of that weapon, similar in form, but more elon-gated (being at least twice as long) was usually made of cariboo horn.

"Apart from the common arrows, the Carriers made use of two other varieties of missiles of Sekanais origin. The heads of both kinds were made from cariboo horn. The first of these, called *krachaenkwaelh* (cut arrow) by the Carriers, was conical in form and not less than 6 inches in length. The broader extremity thereof was hollowed out to receive a wooden shaft which served to dart it off from the bow like a common arrow, with this difference, however, that when in motion the horn point detached itself from the shaft. This projectile was deadly, and intended only for use against an enemy or for killing large game. To shoot smaller game, such as grouse, rabbits, etc., they had recourse to a curiously-wrought triple arrow head consisting of three flat pieces of bone or horn triangular in shape and not unlike the feathers on a sea-otter arrow. These plates were seized to the arrow shaft in several places by sinew passing through the plates and around the wood. The manner of fast-ening to the shaft was similar to that delineated in Morice's fig. 14."

The knives were ordinarily made of the common arrow-head flint, but those of beaver teeth were more esteemed.

"Their arrow, common arrow heads, were of two kinds, bone and flint. The first were made of the front teeth of the beaver, reduced by scraping to the required shape. They were reputed the most effec-tive. Flint arrow-heads were of different sizes, forms, and material. They are produced in Morice's paper for the sake of comparison with those used by the mound-builders of Illinois and other States of the American Union with which they will be found identical in shape and material, though a distance of at least 2,000 miles separate the Abori-gines who made them. He says the 'two marked A and B may be described as the typical arrow-heads of the Western Denes, and are of the blackish resonant flint, generally used in the fabrication of abori-ginal weapons. C and D are composed of a semi-translucent bluish variety of siliceous stone not so common and consequently more prized than the ordinary arrow-flint. E represents the most beautiful of all the Dene arrow-heads in my possession. It has been ingeniously chipped from a hard crystalline species of flint, and its form and finish display evidences of, I should say, exceptionally good workmanship. Some are also formed of a whitish siliceous pebble; but the points made therewith are, as a rule, of a rather rough description.'"

---

* Jones, *S. R.*, 1866, p. 324.

"The regular hunting or war bow of the Tse'kehne was of mountain maple (Acer glabrum, Tow) and 5½ feet or more in length. The edges, both inner and outer, were smoothened over so as to permit of strips of unplaited sinew being twisted around to insure therefor the necessary strength. These pieces of sinew were fastened on with a glue obtained from the sturgeon sound, which also did service for all kinds of gluing purposes among each of the three tribes, while still in their prehistoric period. The central part of the bow, which was so thick as to appear almost rectangular, was finally covered with a tissue of differently-tinged porcupine quills.

"Great care was taken to obtain a bow-string impermeable to snow and rain. With this object in view, delicate threads of sinew were twisted together and afterwards rubbed over with sturgeon glue. This first string was then gradually strengthened by additional sinew threads twisted around the first and main cord, each overlaying of sinew being thoroughly saturated with glue. Finally when the string had attained a sufficient thickness for efficient service it was repeatedly rubbed over with gum of the black pine (*Abies balsamea*).

"A less elaborate bow (fig. 31) is still to this very day in use among the Tse'kehne in connection with the blunt arrow already mentioned. It is of seasoned willow (*Salix longifolia*), and being devoid of any sinew backing or other strengthening device, its edges are more angular than those of fig. 30. Its string consists merely of a double line of cariboo skin slightly twisted together. The specimen figured above measures 4 feet 10 inches.

"The Carrier bow was never much more than 4 feet in length, and the wooden part of it was invariably juniper (*J. occidentalis*). Instead of being twisted around as in the Tse'kehne bow, the threads of sinew were glued on the back after the fashion of the Eskimo bow, with this difference, however, that in the Carrier weapon the sinew was not plaited. When a layer of thin sinew strips had been fastened lengthwise on the entire back of the bow, it was allowed to dry, after which others were successively added until the desired strength had been obtained. A process analogous to that whereby the Tse'kehne bowstring was made was followed in cording the string of the Carrier bow."*

"The most powerful as well as most artistic weapon is the bow. It is made of beech or spruce in three pieces, curving in opposite direction, and ingeniously bound by twisted sinews, so as to give the greatest possible strength. Arrows, as well as spears, lances, and darts, are of white spruce, and pointed with bone, ivory, flint, and slate.

"They have two sorts of bows, arrows pointed with iron, flint, and bone, or blunt for birds. (*Simpson Nar., 123.*)

"They ascended the Mackenzie in former times as far as the Ramparts to obtain flinty slate for lance and arrow-points. (Richardson's *Jour.*, vol. I, p. 213.)

"One weapon was a walrus tooth fixed to the end of a wooden staff. (Beechey's *Voy.*, vol. I, p. 343.)

"At Coppermine River arrows are pointed with slate or copper. (Hearne's *Travels*, pp. 161–169.") †

---

* Father A. G. Morice, *Trans. Canad. Inst.*, Toronto, 1894, IV, 58, 59.

† See Bancroft, *N. R.* vol. I, p. 59.

EXPLANATION OF PLATE XXXVII.

THE MAKING AND MOUNTING OF AN ARROW POINT.

FIG. 1. Knocking off chips from a core of obsidian by means of the stone hammer and pitching tool of antler; one person operating.

FIG. 2. Knocking off chips from a core of obsidian by means of the stone hammer and pitching tool of antler; two persons operating.

FIG. 3. Pressing off flakes from a blade of siliceous stone by means of the bone flaker, the operator holding the blade against the ball of the thumb and pressing from him.

FIG. 4. Pressing off flakes from a blade of siliceous stone by means of a bone flaker, the operator holding the blade on the palm of the hand and pressing downward. Frequently the hand is gloved or a bit of rawhide is first laid upon the palm.

FIG. 5. Pressing off flakes from a bit of siliceous stone by means of the bone flaker, the operator holding the block upon a bit of wood with his left hand and pressing downward with the right. This is a very effectual mode of working.

FIG. 6. Fastening the arrowhead upon the shaft by means of a filament of moist sinew. The shaft is held firmly under the left arm for a bearing, held and revolved by the left hand, and the moist filament of sinew is held tight and guided by the right hand.

PLATE XXXVII.

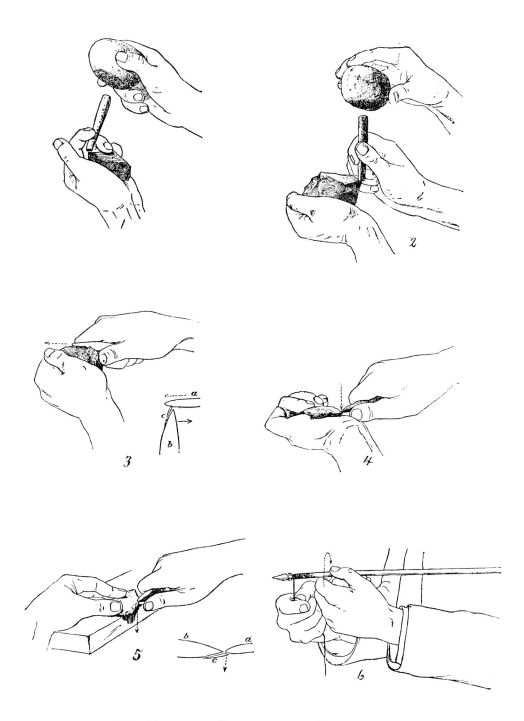

THE MAKING AND MOUNTING OF AN ARROW-POINT.
(After Holmes and Hough.)

EXPLANATION OF PLATE XXXVIII.

MATERIALS OF THE ARROW-MAKER.

This plate shows the typical collection of material as it is prepared for use by the Hupa arrow-maker (Athapascan stock), northern California. The same outfit would do for any other craftsman of this class throughout the temperate regions of North America, only the form of the tool would be changed.

FIG. 1. THE SHAFT. A simple twig or rod or switch of any suitable wood. If the pith be thick, the rod is treated much as a reed. If it be meager the twig may be whittled away at certain parts to change the form. Among certain tribes the arrow shafts are made of sections split from large sticks.

FIG. 2. THE POINT. The material is as varied as stone with conchoidal fracture may be. Spalls are struck off and made into arrowheads by a multitude of processes explained in the text.

FIG. 3. SINEW FOR SEIZING. The figure shows its appearance as it is dried and saved up for future use.

FIG. 4. GUM. The exudations from trees or glue from fish or animal substances used to hold the feather to the shaft, the head in its place, or to smear over the sinew seizing to give it a smooth and homogeneous appearance.

FIG. 5. PAINT MORTAR. The paint mortars of the American aborigines are discoidal stones usually, with a shallow cavity. In this cavity ochers and other paint substances are ground, mixed with the grease of animals or with water, and used in decorating both bows and arrows.

FIG. 6. FEATHERS. The plume is stripped off with a small portion of the midrib, seized to the shaft, and trimmed in many ways.

PLATE XXXVIII.

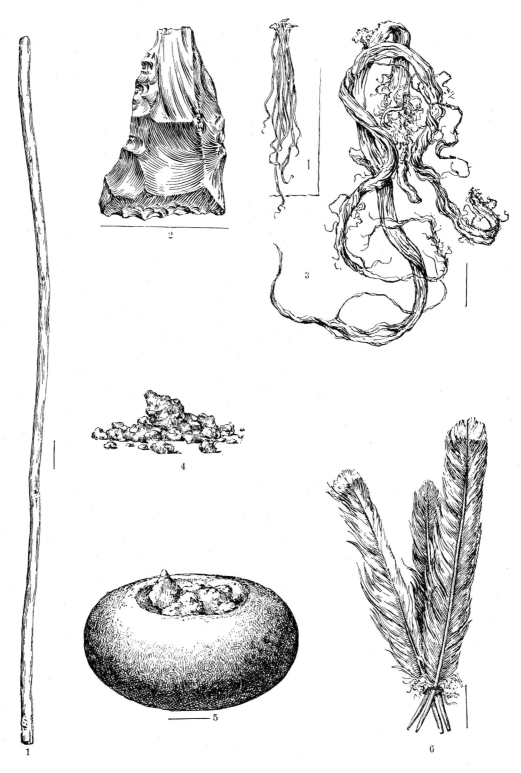

MATERIALS OF THE ARROW-MAKER.

TOOLS OF THE ARROW-MAKER.

This plate shows the tools of the arrow-maker.

FIG. 1. SHAFT STRAIGHTENER. The example figured is from the Hupa (Athapascan) tribe of California. It is a piece of yew ten inches long, spindle-shaped and having an oblong hole through the middle. The arrow shaft is drawn through the hole and straightened by pressure on the ends of the tool.

FIG. 2. THE GLUE STICK, which is simply a bit of wood having one end covered with glue, used like a tinner's soldering iron.

FIGS. 3 and 4. ARROWHEAD CHIPPERS. Showing the primitive method of joining the working parts to the handle. One point is a bit of bone, the other a rod of soft iron, which in this example replaces one of bone or antler.

FIG. 5. THE PITCHING TOOL. A column of antler used like a cold chisel in knocking off spalls or flakes or blades by means of some kind of hammer.

FIGS. 6 and 7. RASPING AND POLISHING STONES. All the American tribes used coarse sandstone for wood rasps, and in the making of arrow shafts cut grooves in the rasp to give rotundity to the wood. The polishing was done with finer sandstone, shagreen, siliceous grass, etc.

FIG. 8. GLUE SHELL. An implement made of muscle shell worn over the finger and employed in smoothing down glue and sinew on bows and arrows.

FIG. 9. SAW. In this example an old case knife blade, hacked on the edge. In primitive times wood saws were made of chipped siliceous stone.

PLATE XXXIX.

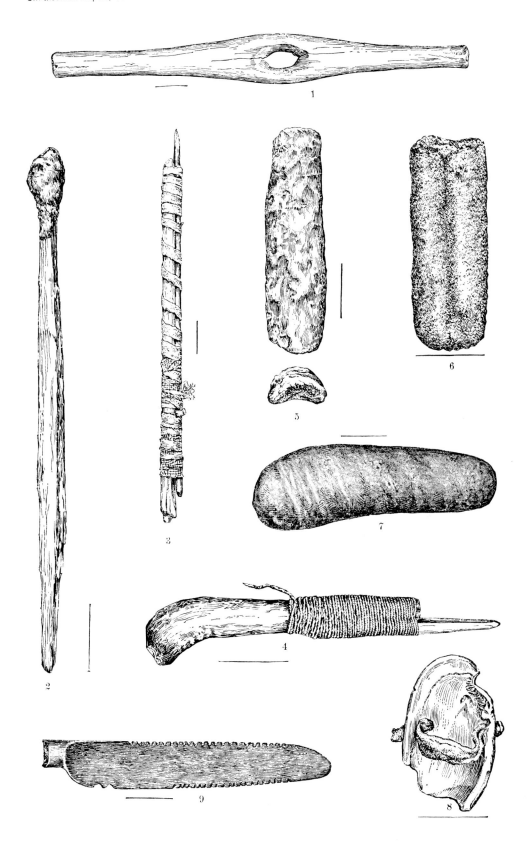

TOOLS OF THE ARROW-MAKER.

EXPLANATION OF PLATE XL.

The Parts of an Arrow.

The dissected arrow is shown in such fashion that the parts of a highly complex example may be understood.

A COMPLETE ARROW. Foreshafted type, found among the tribes of Oregon and northern California.

The ideas made specially prominent are:

FIG. 1. The method of inserting the foreshaft into the end of the shaft.

FIG. 2. The attachment of the head to the barb piece by diagonal lashing of sinew and the union of the stone head with the barb piece of bone attached to the foreshaft.

FIG. 3. The laying on of the feathering in one example having what is called the "rifling" of the arrow.

FIG. 4. The foreshaft before the head is attached, showing especially the neat manner of its union with the shaft.

FIG. 5. The painted bands or ribands of the shaftment, called by a variety of names.

FIG. 6. The relation of the nock to the pithy wood of the shaft.

PLATE XL.

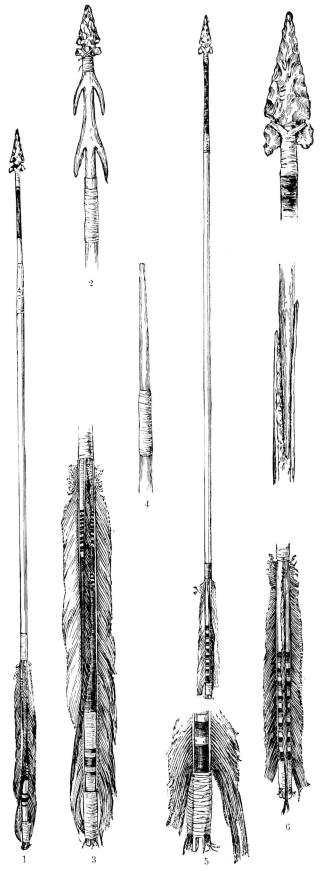

THE PARTS OF AN ARROW.

EXPLANATION OF PLATE XLI.

ARROWS OF SOUTHERN CALIFORNIA AND ARIZONA.

FIG. 1. SHAFT of reed. Foreshaft, a rod of hard wood inserted into the end of the shaft, which is tapered down and seized with sinew. Head, of jasper inserted into a deep notch in the end of the foreshaft and held in place by diagonal lashings of sinew and mesquite gum. Feathers, three, seized at the ends with sinew. Shaft, 26½ inches; foreshaft, 7½ inches.

> Cat. No. 11783, U. S. N. M. Moki Indians, Arizona. Collected by Bureau of Ethnology.

NOTE.—The Moki Indians are of Shoshonean stock, live in pueblos, and use the Mohave type of arrows.

FIG. 2. SHAFT, of reed. Foreshaft, a rod of hard wood inserted into the end of the shaft and seized with sinew. Head of chalcedony, triangular, inserted into a "saw cut" at the end of the foreshaft, and held in place by mesquit gum laid on so as to form an unbroken surface between the foreshaft and the head. The end of the foreshaft is seized with sinew. Shaftment ornamented with a band of red and a spiral band in black. Nock, cylindrical. Notch, U-shaped. Feathers, three, seized with untwisted sinew. Length, 37 inches.

> Cat. No. 1796, U. S. N. M. Mohave Indians, southern California. Collected by Edward Palmer.

NOTE.—To the right of this example is shown a shorter type of feathering and ornamented shaftment by the same tribe.

FIG. 3. SHAFT, rod of hard wood. Head made from a piece of an old pair of scissors inserted into the split end of the shaft. Feathers, three, lashed at the ends with sinew. Nock spreading, and notch a long deep incision. Length of arrow, 25 inches.

> Mohave Indians.

NOTE.—This arrow, though accredited to the Mohave Indians, belongs to a much more northern type, and if properly labeled by the collector shows the effect of commerce and migration.

FIG. 4. SHAFT, a rod of hard wood. Shaftment daubed with bands of red paint. Feathers, three, fastened at the ends with sinew. The nock is cylindrical. The notch, parallel sided. Foreshaft short, of hard wood, inserted neatly into the end of the shaft and daubed with brown paint. Head, of bottle-glass, inserted slightly into the foreshaft and held in place by a diagonal seizing of sinew. Total length, 34½ inches.

> Cat. No. 128431, U. S. N. M. Yuma Indians. Collected by Col. James Stevenson.

FIG. 5. SHAFT, of reed. The shaftment is ornamented with two bands of red paint connected by longitudinal stripes. Feathers, three, seized with sinew. Nock, cylindrical. The sides of the notch are made parallel by cutting into the reed on either side and splitting out a little piece. The point and foreshaft of this arrow are one, made of a piece of hard wood inserted into the reed-shaft and seized with sinew, and at the other extremity sharpened to a long tapering point. Length of shaft, 2 feet 1¾ inches; foreshaft, 12 inches.

> Cat. No. 76176, U. S. N. M. Cocopa Indians, Mexico. Collected by Edward Palmer.

FIG. 6. SHAFT, of reed. Foreshaft, square bit of mesquite wood inserted into the end of the shaft and seized with sinew. Feathers, three, lashed with sinew at the ends. Shaftment ornamented with a band of red. This specimen is rudely made, showing a degenerate art. Length of shaft, 28 inches; foreshaft, 10 inches.

> Cat. No. 9072, U. S. N. M. Yaquis Indians. Collected by Edward Palmer.

PLATE XLI.

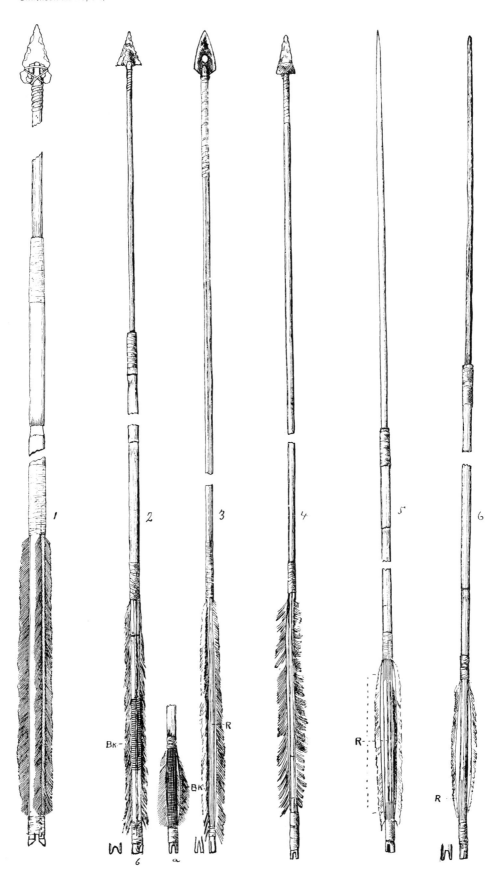

ARROWS OF SOUTHERN CALIFORNIA AND ARIZONA.

EXPLANATION OF PLATE XLII.

ARROWS OF THE PUEBLO REGION AND SOUTHWESTERN UNITED STATES.

FIG. 1. SHAFT, a small stem or twig, with very shallow and sinuous shaft streaks. Feathers, three, loosely held on and seized at either end with sinew. At the edges of the shaftment are bands of brown and black. The nock is slightly spreading. The notch is U-shaped. Point, of iron, leaf-shaped and slender, the tang inserted in a notch at the end of the shaft and seized with sinew. This arrow, like most of those collected from this tribe, is very coarsely made. Total length of shaft, 24½ inches.

> Cat. No. 75678, U. S. N. M. Zuni Indians. Collected by James Stevenson.

FIG. 2. SHAFT, of reed. Foreshaft, a twig, perhaps of greasewood set into the end of the reed of the shaft and seized with sinew. The stone head is sagittate, let into the head of the foreshaft, and fastened first with sinew and then covered with gum. The whole foreshaft is covered with dark gum. Feathers, three, seized at the ends with sinew and trimmed down along the margins. It is possible that these reed arrows of the Oraibi are derived from the Mohave or Apache further south. Length, shaft, 24 inches; foreshaft, 12 inches.

> Cat. No. 11780, U. S. N. M. Hopi or Moki pueblo of Oraibi (Shoshonean) Arizona. Collected by J. W. Powell.

FIG. 3. SHAFT, of twig; shaft streaks very wavy and crowded. In comparison with the size of the arrow the feathers are very wide and conspicuous. They are laid close to the shaftment and are seized with sinew. The nock is slightly expanding. Notch, angular; head of jasper, small, inserted into the end of the shaft and seized with a diagonal lashing of sinew, which passes also once transversely. Total length, 26 inches. Especial attention is called to the existence of the reed arrow (fig. 2) and the simple arrow in the same pueblo.

> Cat. No. 22594, U. S. N. M. Hopi or Moki Indians, Arizona. Collected by Maj. J. W. Powell.

FIG. 4. SHAFT, a single rod bluntly pointed at the head and seized with sinew. Feathers, three, neatly seized with sinew at the fore end and by seven narrow bands of sinew behind. The feathers are far from the nock, which is also bound with sinew. This type of feathering is rare in America. Length, 30 inches.

> Cat. No. 165573, U. S. N. M. Pima Indians, Salado Valley, Arizona. Collected by F. Webb Hodge.

FIG. 5. This arrow is similar to that shown in fig. 4, but differing from it in having a small stone head wrapped crosswise, in having the feathers nearer the nock, and in the omission of the intervening wrappings of sinew on the feather.

> Cat. No. 76021, U. S. N. M. Pima Indians. Collected by Dr. Edward Palmer.

PLATE XLII.

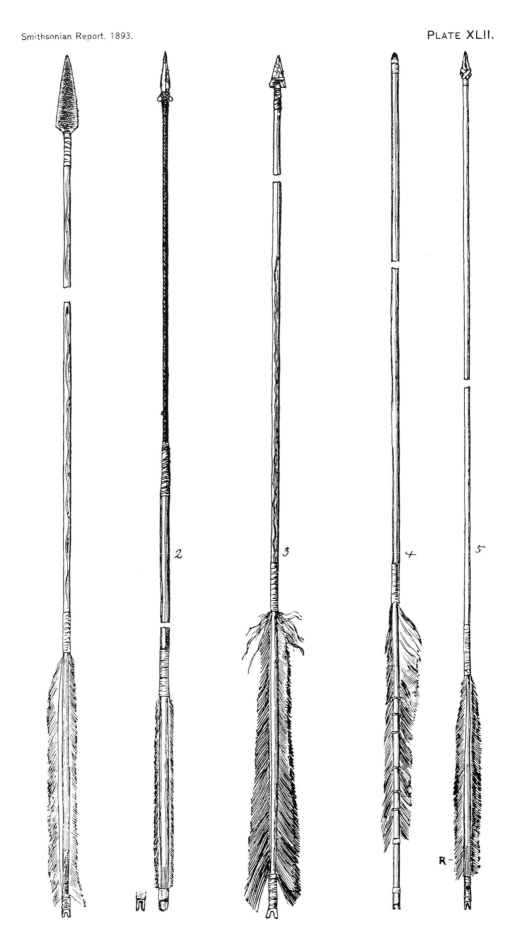

ARROWS OF THE PUEBLO REGION AND SOUTHWESTERN UNITED STATES.

EXPLANATION OF PLATE XLIII.

ARROWS OF APACHE TRIBES, SOUTHWESTERN UNITED STATES.

Fig. 1. The shaft is of osier, with shaft streaks nearly straight. Shaftment tapering backwards and banded with red and green paint. Nock, swallow-tail shaped. Feathers, three, seized at their ends with sinew and extending off from the shaft at the middle. The front part of the feathering is ornamented with tufts of down. The delicate blade of iron forming the head is inserted into a "saw cut" in the end of the shaft and seized with sinew. Total length, 25½ inches.

> Cat. No. 6964, U. S. N. M. Comanche Indians, of Texas. Collected by Dr. E. Palmer, U. S. Army.

Fig. 2. SHAFT, of reed. The shaftment is ornamented with bands of red and black. Feathers, three, seized with sinew. Notch, parallel-sided. The foreshaft, of hard wood, fits into the end of the reed shaft and is seized with sinew. It is daubed with brown paint. Head, of jasper, incurved at the base and notched on the sides. It is inserted into the end of the foreshaft and fastened by a diagonal seizing of sinew and further secured by mesquite gum. Total length of shaft, 37½ inches.

> Cat. No. 5519, U. S. N. M. Apache Indians, of Arizona. Collected by Dr. Edward Palmer.

Fig. 3. SHAFT, of rhus, painted red. Feathers, three, seized with sinew, standing off from the shaftment. The nock is cylindrical and the notch is rectangular. Head, of old hoop iron, inserted in a notch in the end of the shaft and seized with sinew. This specimen is very roughly made. The total length of the shaft is 25 inches.

> Cat. No. 25512, U. S. N. M. Apache Indians. Collected by Dr. J. B. White, U. S. Army.

Fig. 4. SHAFT, of hard wood. Iron head let in at the end of the shaft. Feathers, three, seized with sinew. Shaft painted blue. Shaftment bound with yellow, blue, and red streaks. Length, shaft, 2 feet 4 inches.

> Cat. No. 130307, U. S. N. M. Apache Indians, Athapascan stock, Arizona. Collected by Dr. T. C. Scantling, U. S. Army.

Fig. 5. SHAFT, of osier. Has three shaft streaks, two nearly straight and one a wavy line. The shaftment is ornamented with bands of red and blue. Feathers, three, attached at their ends by a seizing of sinew and glued to the shaft. Near the seizing is a bunch of downy feathers, left for the purpose of ornamentation. Nock, widely spread. Notch, angular. The head is a tapering blade of iron, a portion of which, with the tang, is inserted into a "saw cut" and neatly seized with sinew. Total length, 27 inches.

Fig. 6. This arrow is similar to No. 5 A, excepting a little ornamentation on the front of the shaft. Total length, 24½ inches.

NOTE.—Both of these arrows are perfect of their kind. It is difficult to conceive how a more deadly missile could be made.

> Cat. No. A and B 150450, U. S. N. M. Navajo Indians. Collected by Dr. Washington Matthews, U. S. Army.

PLATE XLIII.

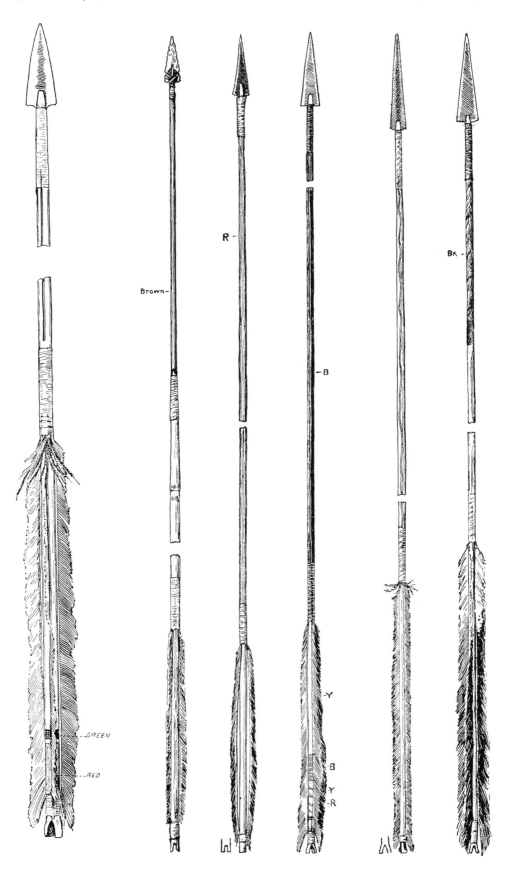

ARROWS OF APACHE TRIBES, SOUTHWESTERN UNITED STATES.

EXPLANATION OF PLATE XLIV.

ARROWS FROM VARIOUS TRIBES OF THE GREAT INTERIOR BASIN.

FIG. 1. SHAFT, of rhus. Shaftment painted with red and brown paint. Feathers, three, laid on close to the shaftment and neatly seized with sinew. The nock is cylindrical and the notch U-shaped. Head, of chalcedony, inserted into a shallow notch at the end of the shaftment, seized with sinew, and afterward cemented with mesquite gum. This is a beautifully made specimen. Total length of shaft, 27 inches.

Cat. No. 14699, U. S. N. M. Piute Indians. Collected by Major J. W. Powell.

FIG. 2. SHAFT, of hard wood, trimmed down. Head, of hoop iron, fastened on with lashing of thread. Feathers, three, seized with sinew, glued down and trimmed along the margins. Nock, swallow-tailed, and the feathering extends beyond the nock. Length, shaft, 2 feet 3 inches.

Cat. No. 131238, U. S. N. M. Shoshonean. Collected by G. Brown Goode.

FIG. 3. Gambling arrow of the Apache Indians. Shaft, painted blue; three tolerably straight blood streaks. Feathers, three, seized with sinew. Nock in form of swallow's tail. Notch, acute angular. The point of wood is a continuation of the shaft, triangular in cross-section. The ornamentation on the point consists of lozenge-shaped cavities and furrows filled with red and blue paint. In a series of these arrows no two are ornamented exactly alike. Used in divination and gambling. Mr. Frank H. Cushing connects the divination by throwing a bunch of these arrows with the position of the arrows in the Assyrian cuneiform inscriptions.

Cat. No. 73268, U. S. N. M. Apache Indians. Collected by G. H. Leigh.

FIG. 4. A rude unfinished arrow with shaft unstraightened. Three feathers loosely attached to the shaft with sinew, the whole showing the degeneration of the art of arrow-making in ceremonial usages.

Cat. No. 1496, U. S. N. M.

FIG. 5. SHAFT, of rhus. Feathers, three, seized with sinew. Nock, cylindrical; notch, angular. There is no head. Length, 23½ inches.

Cat. No. 22287, U. S. N. M. Bannock Indians, Idaho. Collected by W. H. Danilson.

FIG. 6. SHAFT, of osier. Blood streaks, slightly wavy. Feathers, three, seized with sinew. It is difficult to say whether they were formerly glued to the shaftment or not. Shaftment, cylindrical. Notch, angular. Head of iron inserted into the end of the shaft and seized with sinew. In other specimens from the same tribe stone heads are found fastened on with a diagonal lashing of sinew. Total length, 26 inches.

Cat. No. 9048, U. S. N. M. Snake Indians, Idaho. Collected by Dr. C. Moffat.

PLATE XLIV.

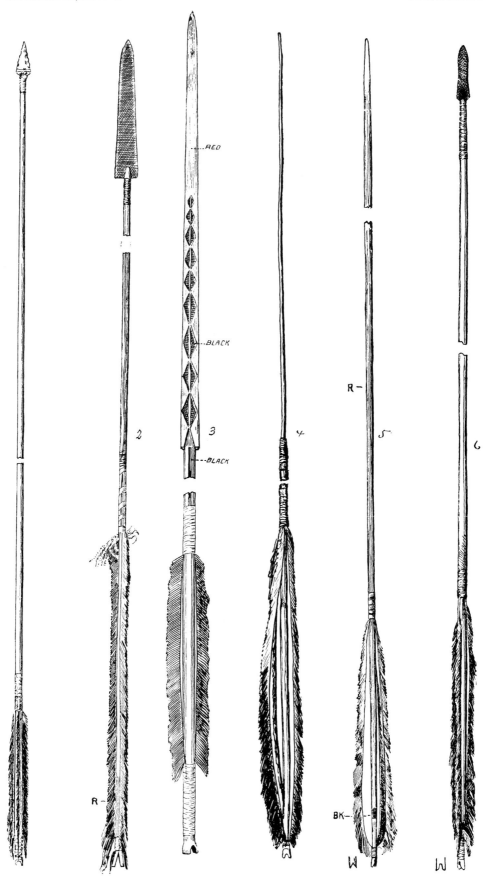

ARROWS FROM VARIOUS TRIBES OF THE GREAT INTERIOR BASIN.

Arrows of Caddoan Tribes, Texas and northward.

Fig. 1. A simple rod or twig from which the arrow shaft is made. It was collected from one of the Indian tribes in the buffalo-hunting regions, and might have been the groundwork of any of the arrows upon this and the preceding plate.

Fig. 2. The shaft of this arrow is a twig of osier; the shaft streaks two, straight. The shaftment is banded with blue, green, red, and yellow. Feathers three, laid on flat and seized with sinew at the ends. The edges are shorn, so as to give the arrows a neat appearance. The nock is spreading; notch, angular. Head, leaf-shaped, of hoop iron, inserted into a deep notch at the end of the shaft and seized with sinew. Total length of shaft, 27½ inches.

> Cat. No. 8461, U. S. N. M. Tonkawa Indians, Texas. Collected by Dr. McElderry, U. S. Army.

Fig. 3. Shaft, a slender rod of hard wood. Feathers, three, held in place by seizing with sinew and trimmed straight on the edge. Nock expanding and blood streaks straight and zigzag. Length, 2 feet 1 inch.

> Cat. No. 6965, U. S. N. M. Wichita Indians, Caddoan stock. Collected by E. Palmer.

Fig. 4. Shaft, of hard wood; head let into the end of the shaft and seized with sinew. Feathers, three, long, and glued down and seized smoothly at the ends with sinew. Nock, fish-tail. Shaft streaks, three in number, deep and sinuous. Length of shaft, 2 feet 1 inch.

> Cat. No. 130795, U. S. N. M. Pawnee Indians, Caddoan stock, Nebraska. Collected by E. F. Bernard.

Fig. 5. Shaft, a delicate twig, with blood streaks consisting of wavy furrows. Feathers, three, seized down with sinew and glued to the shaftment. Edges trimmed so as to form parallel lines. The front of the shaftment is ornamented with broad green bands. The shaftment is trimmed away at its extremity so as to leave the nock a cylindrical bulb. The notch is U-shaped. The head is a blade of iron inserted into a "saw cut" at the end of the shaft. The tang is serrated along the barb, securing the more effectual fastening of the head. Total length of shaft, 25 inches.

> Cat. No. 129873, U. S. N. M. Pawnee Indians. Collected by H. M. Creel.

PLATE XLV.

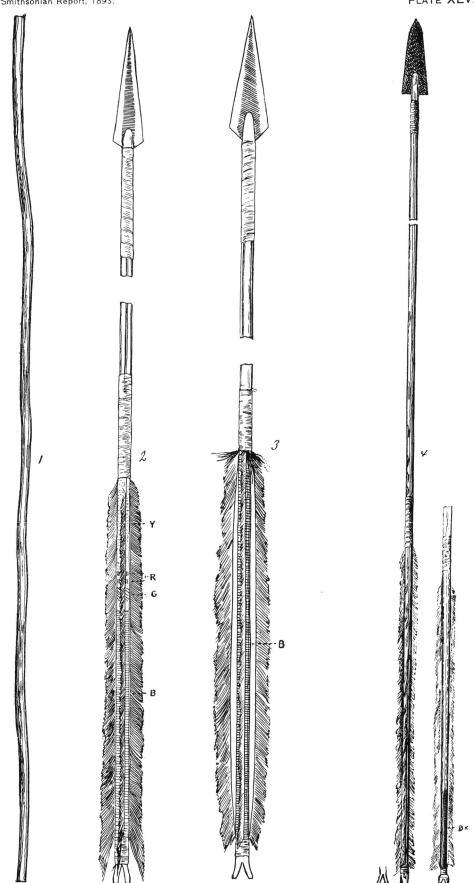

ARROWS OF CADDOAN TRIBES, TEXAS AND NORTHWARD.

SIOUAN ARROWS, DAKOTA TRIBES.

FIG. 1. SHAFT, of osier. Shaftment, banded with red. Feathers, three, seized with sinew at the end and shorn neatly on the outer edges. Near the nock of the arrow is an ornamental feather in the feathering, produced by leaving the plume on both sides of the rib of the feather for about an inch, so that the arrow at this point appears to have six feathers. The nock is slightly spreading; notch, U-shaped. No head. Total length of shaft, 27¾ inches.

  Cat. No. 21286, U. S. N. M. Sioux Indians, Minnesota. Collected by Rev. Geo. Ainslie.

FIG. 2. On this arrow a pyramidal piece of bone serves for a head, and the shaftment is striped with blue and red. This specimen is figured for the purpose of showing oddities of form since the adoption of the rifle. Neither of these arrows, probably, was ever used. Among the Plains Indians the iron arrowhead was introduced many years ago, and samples with stone heads are extremely rare and quite open to suspicion. Length, 24 inches.

  Cat. No. 8439, U. S. N. M. Sioux Indians, Fort Berthold. Collected by Drs. Gray and Matthews, U. S. Army.

FIG. 3. SHAFT, a rod of osier; blood streaks, very jagged. Feathers, three, seized with sinew, loosely wrapped, glued to the shaftment, and there are streaks of blue paint drawn between the featherings. The nock is bulbous; the notch is widely angular. Head, of chalcedony, notched on the sides and glued into a notch in the end of the shaft. The seizing is gone from this arrow, but the notches in the side of the head, as well as the clean appearance of the shaft, indicate that it was once present.

FIG. 4. SHAFTMENT, a delicate rod of osier; blood streaks, wavy. Shaftment tapering toward the nock. Feathers, three, seized at the end with sinew and standing off from the shaftment. Nock, slightly expanding; notch, swallow-tail-shaped. Head, a piece of wire driven into the end of the shaft, very neatly seized with sinew, and sharpened at the point. Length, 26 inches.

  Cat. No. 2466, U. S. N. M. Sioux Indians. Collected by Dr. Washington Matthews, U. S. Army.

FIG. 5. SHAFT, of osier. Shaftment, banded with red. Feathers, three, seized at each end with sinew and glued. The nock is swallowtail-shaped; notch, angular. In the arrows of the Sioux the nock is usually very much widened out at the extremity, giving the warrior a firm grip in releasing. Head, of obsidian, rudely chipped and inserted into the notch in the end of the shaft. In the companion to this arrow the blood streaks are slightly jagged. The head is of white jasper and the feather is 10½ inches long. Length, 24 inches. Length of feathers, 10 inches.

  Cat. No. 8439, U. S. N. M. Sioux Indians. Collected by Gray and Matthews, U. S. Army.

PLATE XLVI.

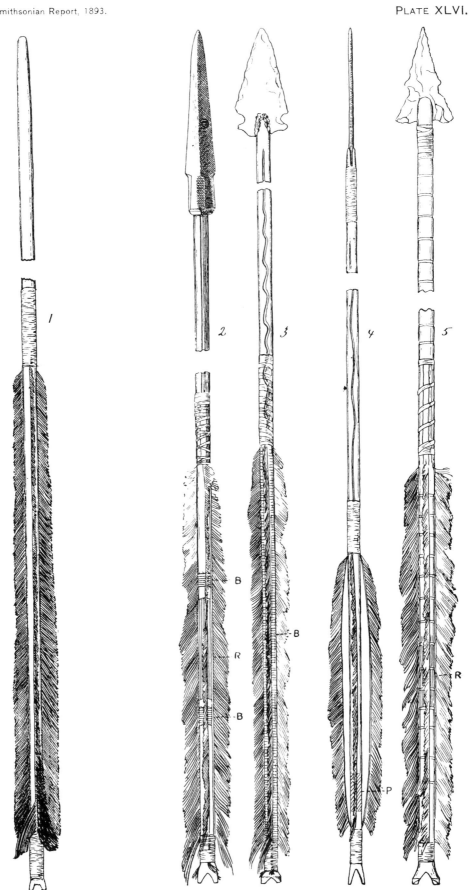

SIOUAN ARROWS, DAKOTA TRIBES.

EXPLANATION OF PLATE XLVII.

Siouan Arrows, Nebraska and Dakota.

FIG. 1. SHAFT, of osier. The shaftment is decorated with alternate bands of red, blue, and yellow. The shaftment is cut away at the outer end so as to leave the nock a projecting cylinder and give a better grip to the fingers in discharging the arrow. Notch, U-shaped. The head, a slender blade of iron let into a "saw cut" in the end of the shaft, the two lips of this cut being shaved down neatly so as to form no impediment to the progress of the arrow. This is a very delicate and effective weapon. The iron blade is slightly barbed at the base. Length of shaft, 26 inches.

> Cat. No. 76831, U. S. N. M. Sioux Indians, Nebraska. Collected by Governor Furness.

FIG. 2. SHAFT, of hard wood. Shaftment ornamented with yellow and red bands. Feathers, seized with sinew, held on spirally, and glued to the shaftment. It is difficult to say whether this spiral arrangement was designed to make the arrow spin through the air. Authorities differ on this point, and the object of direct flight at close range would be more than canceled by the disadvantage of untangling a revolving arrowhead in the hair of the buffalo or deer. The nock is bulbous; notch, angular. Head, a diamond-shaped blade of sheet iron, inserted into the end of the shaft, and seized with sinew. Length of feathers, 7½ inches; total length of shaft, 26 inches.

> Cat. No. 131356, U. S. N. M. Collected by Mrs. A. C. Jackson.

FIG. 3. SHAFT, of hard wood; point of iron, long triangle, inserted into the saw cut in the head and seized with sinew. Feathers, three, glued on, seized at the ends with sinew and trimmed down. The shaftment is ornamented with a blue band. The nock is fish-tail pattern. Shaft streaks sinuous. Other arrows from this same tribe have different colored bands in the shaftment. Length of shaft, 2 feet 3 inches.

> Cat. No. 8418, U. S. N. M. Gros Ventres, Siouan stock. Collected by Dr. Matthews, U. S. Army.

FIG. 4. Blood streaks, quite straight. Feathers, three, glued to the shaft, and seized with sinew. The strips of sinew with which the Sioux Indians lash their featherings are much broader than those used by the West Coast Indians, and very often are laid on like an open spiral or coil. The feathers are shorn. Nock, spreading; notch, shallow. Head, diamond-shaped, the margins of the inner half being filed like a saw. The head is inserted in the end of the shaft and seized with sinew. Total length of shaft, 25 inches.

> Cat. No. 23736, U. S. N. M. Sioux Indians, Devil's Lake. Collected by Paul Beckwith.

FIG. 5. Example of arrows from the Sioux Indians by the U. S. Weather Bureau. This large number of arrows promiscuously gathered affords an excellent opportunity for studying the lines within which the bands and tribes of the same family vary their arrows. The shafts are all slender, made of hard wood. Some have shaft streaks, others none. They vary also in the number of streaks on the shaft and their form, whether straight, sinuous, or zigzag. These arrows differ also in the length and form of the points, in the length, attachment, and ornamentation of the feather, but all have the wide fish-tail nock, and this seems to be an unvarying quality in Sioux arrows.

> Cat. No. 154016, U. S. N. M. Sioux Indians, Siouan stock. Collected by M. M. Hazen.

PLATE XLVII.

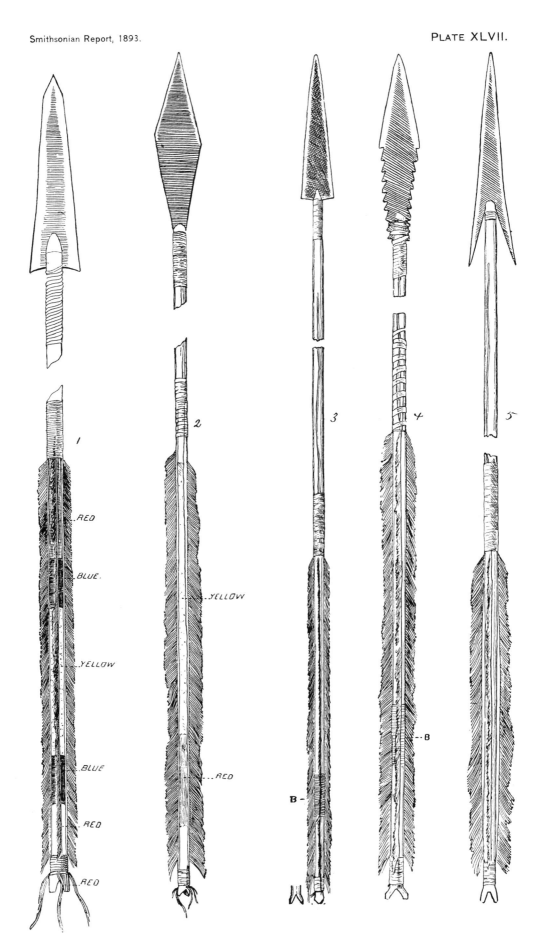

SIOUAN ARROWS, NEBRASKA AND DAKOTA.

ARROWS OF NORTHERN CALIFORNIA AND OREGON

FIG. 1. SHAFT, beautifully smoothed. Shaftment painted deep red. Feathers, three, glued on, and delicately seized at either end with sinew. The ends of the feathers project at least an inch beyond the notch. The nock is cylindrical; notch, U-shaped. Head, of obsidian, leaf-shaped, with notches near the base, let into a notch at the end of the shaft, seized with sinew and transparent glue. Total length of shaft, 31½ inches.

> Cat. No. 2807, U. S. N. M. Oregon Indians. Collected by Lieut. Wilkes, U. S. Navy.

FIG. 2. SHAFT, of rhus. Shaftment, striped with black, red, and brown. Feathers, seized at the end with sinew, standing off from the shaftment, and shorn quite close to the midrib. Nock, cylindrical; notch, U-shaped. Foreshaft, of hard wood, painted red, sharpened, inserted into the end of the shaft, and seized with sinew. Head, an extremely delicate point of obsidian, triangular, inserted into a notch in the end of the shaft, and seized with sinew diagonally laid on notches on the sides of the arrowhead. Total length of shaft, 30 inches.

> Cat. No. 15127, U. S. N. M. Northern California. Collected by Wm. Rich.

FIG. 3. SHAFT, a slender twig of rhus, striped with red and blue at its upper extremity. The shaftment is ornamented with zigzag lines in the same colors. Feathers, three, glued to the shaftment and seized at either end with sinew. Nock, cylindrical; notch, very slight. Head, of obsidian, slender, sagittate in form; the tang inserted in a slit at the extremity of the shaft and seized with sinew. This shaft has a barb of very narrow regular grooves around the upper extremity, as though produced by a lathe. This feature is common to many California arrows. Total length of shaft, 29 inches.

> Cat. No. 126517, U. S. N. M. Hupa Indians, California. Collected by Capt. P. H. Ray, U. S. Army.

FIG. 4. SHAFT, a rod. Shaftment, striped with green. Feathers, three, seized at the ends with sinew and laid flat on the shaftment. Nock, cylindrical; notch, U-shaped. Head, of gray chert, long, and delicately inserted in the end of the shaft by a seizing which passes around the deep notches at the sides. Total length, 34 inches. The shafts of the California arrows are of wild currant, rhus, willow, and other straight twig-like stalks.

> Cat. No. 131110, U. S. N. M. Pitt Indians, California. Collected by N. J. Purcell.

FIG. 5. SHAFT, a rod; striped with narrow bands of blue and red and the natural color of the wood. Feathers, three, neatly shorn, seized with sinew and glued fast to the shaftment. The sinew is colored with a red paint resembling shellac. Nock, cylindrical; notch, shallow. Foreshaft, of hard wood, painted blue, inserted in the end of the shaft and seized with sinew. In many of the California arrows the foreshafts have been revolved between two coarse pieces of sandstone, or by means of a file cut so as to give the appearance of being neatly seized with very fine thread. It also confers a suspicion of machinery on some of these later examples. The head is of jasper, triangular, delicate, tapering, deeply notched on the side, and held in place by a diagonal lashing of sinew. Other specimens from the same quiver have heads of chalcedony, the edges of which are beautifully serrated. Total length, 31 inches.

> Cat. No. 126517, U. S. N. M. Hupa Indians, California. Collected by P. H. Ray.

FIG. 6. This figure shows the variety of arrow points in use among the Indians of Upper California. Glass, obsidian, steel, iron points, and wooden foreshaft sharpened, together with others in the same plate, give an understanding of the various ways of attaching the arrowhead to the shaft and foreshaft.

PLATE XLVIII.

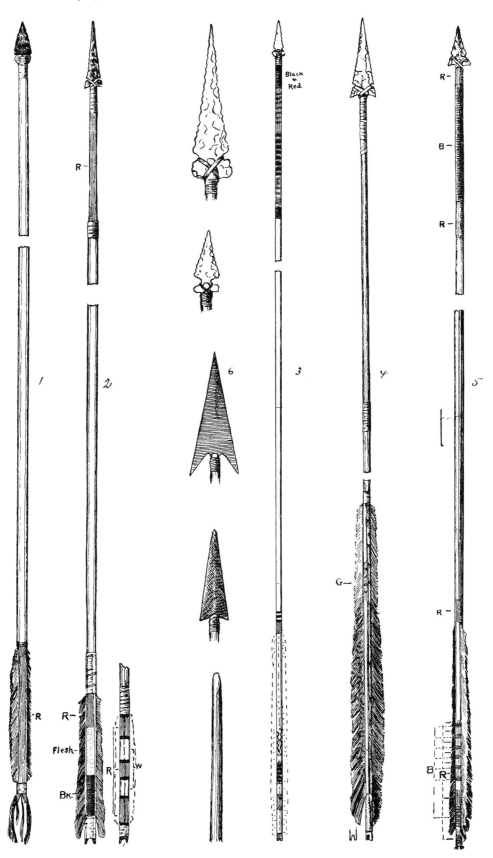

ARROWS OF NORTHERN CALIFORNIA AND OREGON.

EXPLANATION OF PLATE XLIX.

Arrows of Pacific States, from California to Washington.

Fig. 1. The shaft is spindle-shaped, tapering to the nock. Feathers, two, held on flat and seized with pack thread. Nock, expanding; notch, angular. Head, a bit of iron wire, inserted in the end of the shaft, which has been pointed for the purpose, and expanded at the end into a leaf-shaped blade. In some samples the barbs have been cut into this leaf shape partly by means of a filing, to enable the hunter to retrieve his game the better. The total length of the shaft is 28 inches.

Cat. No. 127872, U. S. N. M. Quinaielt Indians, State of Washington. Collected by C. Willoughby.

Fig. 2. Similar to fig. 1 in every respect, excepting the point. There are endless varieties in these.

Fig. 3. Stem, a single rod or twig. Point of brown bottle glass inserted into a notch in the end of the shaft and held in place by a broad band of sinew. Feathers, three, seized at the end with sinew. Shaftment painted red. The notch similar to those of the Chinese arrows. Length of arrow, 31¾ inches.

Cat. No. 76021, U. S. N. M. Tribe unknown, probably Central California.

Fig. 4. Shaft, of spruce. Feathers, three, seized with sinew. Nock, cylindrical; notch, angular. The point is a slender spindle of hard wood inserted into the end of the shaft, seized with sinew, and sharpened at the point. This is a very delicate and effective weapon. Total length, 25 inches.

Cat. No. 649, U. S. N. M. Klamath Indians, California. Collected by George Gibbs.

Fig. 5. Shaft, of twig. Shaftment striped with narrow bands of red and blue. Feathers, three, glued to the shaftment. Nock, cylindrical; notch, very shallow. The head consists of a stone blade and a barb piece of bone. The barb piece is inserted in the end of the shaft and seized with sinew. The barbs are ¾ of an inch long. The stone blade, of red jasper, is fastened to the bone barb piece by a diagonal lashing of sinew. This device is for the purpose of retrieving. If shot into a fish it enables the hunter to secure the animal and free the arrow. If shot at a burrowing animal and the creature escapes into its hole the hunter has a means of recovering the game. Total length of shaft, 30 inches. The adjoining figure on the left is of the same type with different ribbon.

Cat. Nos. 21353, 126576, U. S. N. M. Uroc Indians. Collected by Stephen Powers.

Fig. 6. Shaft, of reed. Shaftment painted white. Feathers, three, 4¾ inches long, seized with sinew. The notch, a shallow cut. Foreshaft, of hard wood. Head, of obsidian, let into the end of the foreshaft and neatly fastened with gum, which is molded to conform to the lines of the arrowhead and to impede as little as possible its flight. This arrow is very neatly made. Length of shaft, 33 inches.

Cat. No. 19709, U. S. N. M. Indians, of Tule River, California. Collected by Stephen Powers.

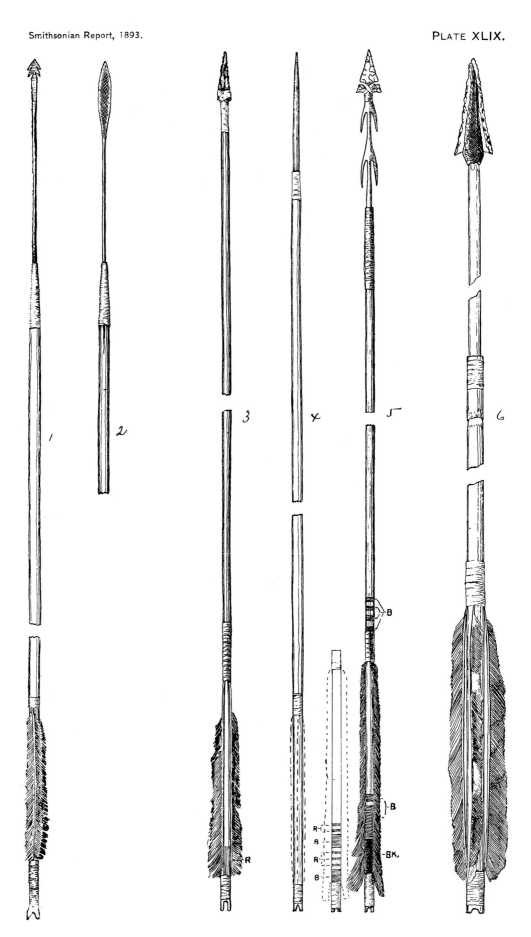

ARROWS OF PACIFIC STATES, FROM CALIFORNIA TO WASHINGTON.

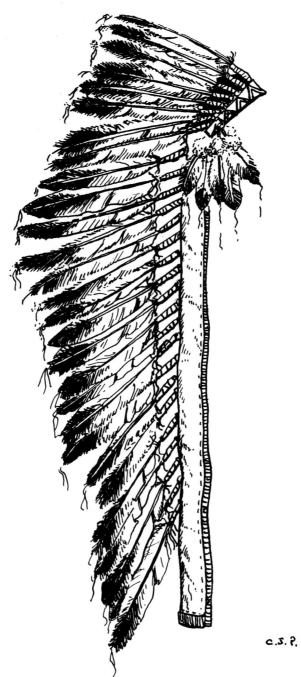

EXPLANATION OF PLATE L.

ARROWS OF TRIBES ABOUT PUGET SOUND, WASHINGTON, AND BRITISH COLUMBIA.

FIG. 1. SHAFT, of cedar. No feathers. Head, a triangular piece of hoop iron inserted into the end of the shaft and seized with twisted sinew. The shaft is ornamented with a spiral band of black. Length of shaft, 32½ inches.

> Cat. No. 650, U. S. N. M. Makah Indians, Cape Flattery. Collected by J. G. Swan.

FIG. 2. SHAFT, of spruce. Head, of iron, inserted into split end of the shaft. Seized with sinew cord. Feathers, three, lashed on with sinew thread. Nock, expanding. Length of arrow, 30 inches.

> Cat. No. 650, U. S. N. M. Makah Indians, Cape Flattery. Collected by George. Gibbs.

FIG. 3. SHAFT, of cedar, tapering both ways from the middle. Seized at the front end with birch bark. Into this end is driven one or more barbed points, of brass or iron wire, pounded flat at the point. One or two barbs filed upon the edges. Feathers, two, laid on flat and seized in place by spruce or birch bark. The nock expands gradually from the feather to the end, where it is spread conspicuously. The noticeable features of this arrow are the following: First, the barbed metallic points taking the place of the ancient bone barbs of Wilkes's time; second, the seizing by means of narrow ribbons of spruce or birch bark; third, the feathers laid on flat, after the fashion of the Eskimo; fourth, exaggerated widening of the butt of the arrow at the nock. There are many specimens of this type in the National Museum. Length: shaft, 2 feet 11 inches; foreshaft, 6½ inches.

> Cat. No. 72656, U. S. N. M. Makah Indians, Wakashan stock, Washington. Collected by J. G. Swan.

FIG. 4. Similar to fig. 3, with difference in shape of metal point.

FIG. 5. SHAFT, spindle-shaped. Feathers, two, laid flat, after the manner of the Eskimo, and seized with narrow strips of bark. Nock, angular, long; ornamented with a wrapping of red flannel, the end of the feather being at least two inches from the end of the arrow. It widens out very rapidly toward the end. Notch, angular. The point, a long spindle of bone with its shallow barbs on one side inserted in a cavity at the end of the shaft and neatly seized with bark. Total length of shaft, 28 inches.

> Cat. No. 76295, U. S. N. M. Makah Indians, Wakashan stock. Collected by J. G. Swan.

FIG. 6. SHAFT, of cedar. Feathers, three, 10 inches long, closely shorn, seized with strips of bark and a bird's feather nicely laid on. The shaft of the arrow is thickest in the middle and tapers in both directions toward the nock where it is smallest, widening out toward the end. Nock, angular. Two points of wood are fastened to the end of the shaft with a neat seizing of bark. In this sample one point is much longer than in the other and the barbs are on the outside. Length, 30 inches.

FIG. 7. SHAFT, similar to that of fig. 6, but there is a single point of bone with barbs on one side. Feathers, two, laid on flat at their ends. Feathering and nock have a separate seizing of bark. Length, 27 inches.

Other samples in the same quiver are quite similar in characteristics, with variations in the barbs.

> Cat. No. 2790, U. S. N. M. State of Washington. Collected by Capt. Charles Wilkes.

FIG. 8. Quite similar to fig. 6 in general form, but the two feathers are laid on flat and spirally. The nock, however, is much ruder, and the point is a long delicate piece of bone, with small barbs on both sides, inserted into the split end of the shaft and seized with bark. Length, 32½ inches.

Cat. No. 2787, U. S. N. M. Columbia River, Oreg. Collected by Capt. Charles Wilkes.

C.S.?

PLATE L.

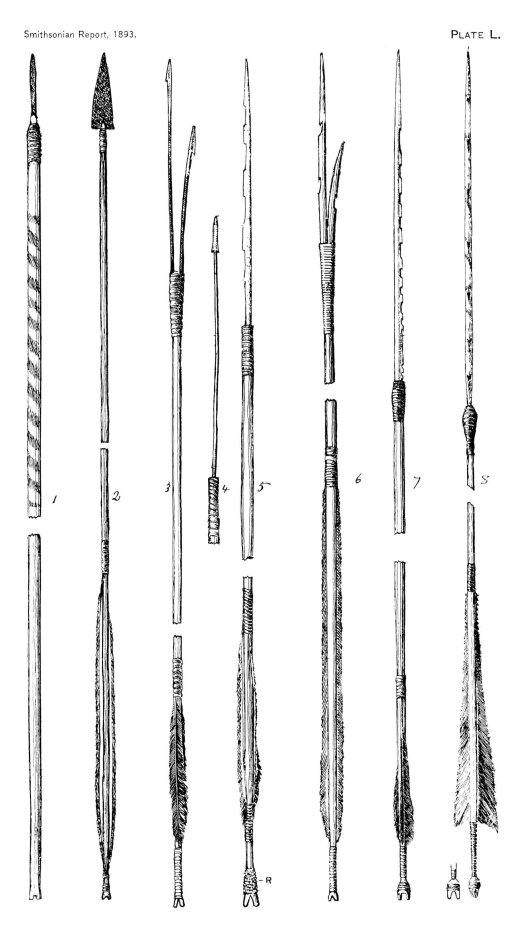

ARROWS OF TRIBES ABOUT PUGET SOUND, WASHINGTON AND BRITISH COLUMBIA.

EXPLANATION OF PLATE LI.

FIGS. 1 and 2. Four examples of Tlingit arrowheads, three of them with barbed pieces to which the metal heads are riveted. These arrowheads have two functions—that of retrieving the game and that of parting easily from the shaft and rankling in the victim until it dies. These should be compared carefully with stone heads in Old World specimens having very long barbs.

FIG. 3. All in one piece; which widens out into a large cone to form a head; slightly expanding at the nock. The notch is formed by cutting off the end of the arrow into an expanding wedge and then making a very shallow incision across the edge. Painted brown and streaked with red. Length, 38 inches.

> Cat. No. 63551, U. S. N. M. Sitka, Alaska. Collected by J. J. McLean.

FIG. 4. SHAFT, of cedar, tapering in two directions. The head is formed of a piece of wire sharpened at one end and driven into the shaft. The other end is flattened and filed to a barb on one side. Similar to fig. 4, Pl. L.

> Cat. No. 73547, U. S. N. M. Haidas, Queen Charlotte Islands. Collected by J. G. Swan.

FIG. 5. Similar to fig. 6, excepting the point is of shell.

FIG. 6. SHAFT, of cedar. Foreshaft let in with a wedge-shaped dowel. Head, a thin sheet of bone, sagittate. Feathers, three, fastened at the ends with sinew covered with glue. Nock somewhat flat, as in the Eskimo arrow. The noticeable features of this arrow are the thin head of bone, the foreshaft, let into the shaft and the flattening nock. Length of shaft, 21 inches; foreshaft, 6 inches.

> Cat. No. 20694, U. S. N. M. Bella Coola Indians, Salishan stock, B. C. Collected by J. G. Swan.

FIG. 7. SHAFT, of cedar, tapering both ways from the middle. Shaftment painted black. Feathers, three, seized at each end with sinew and glued fast to the shaftment. Nock, bulbous; notch, U-shaped. Foreshaft, of hard wood neatly doweled into the end of the cedar shaft, seized with sinew, and painted black. The head is a minutely-barbed thin blade of iron, inserted into the foreshaft and seized with sinew. These are the smallest metal arrow-heads found on any arrow in the world. This arrow was found in Mr. Catlin's collection, after his death, without the name of the tribe; but the wood and the delicate finish point to Oregon as its source. Total length, 32 inches.

> Not numbered. Oregon. Collected by Mr. Catlin.

PLATE LI.

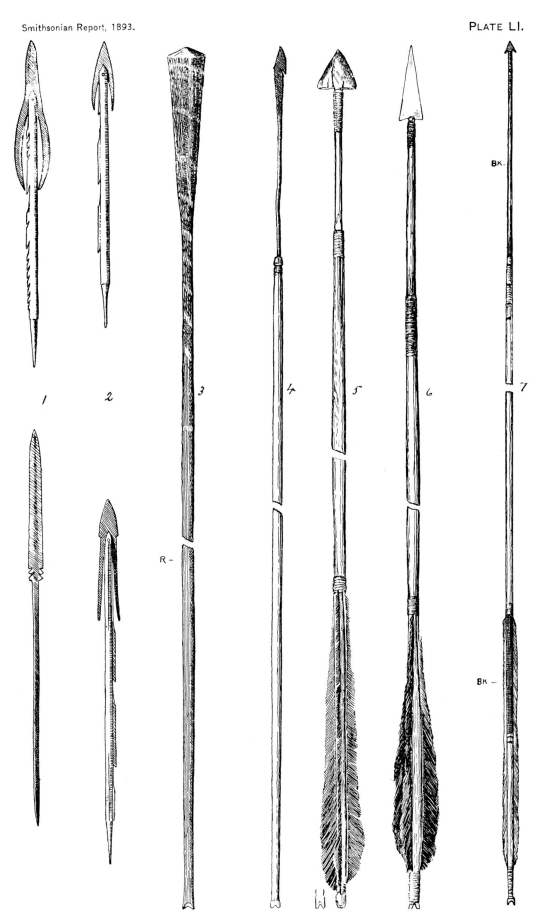

ARROWS OF SOUTHEASTERN ALASKA AND WESTERN BRITISH COLUMBIA.

BARBED AND HARPOON ARROWS OF THE ESKIMO ABOUT THE ALASKAN PENINSULA.

FIG. 1. SHAFT, of cedar, 23½ inches long and ½ inch thick. A streak of red around the middle and either end. The shaftment is somewhat flat, and ornamented with two narrow streaks of red and one bright streak of blue. Feathers, three, two black and one banded brown and white; the ends inserted into slits cut in the shaft and seized with sinew poorly laid on. The middle portions of the feathers are not glued to the arrow. The nock is flat, in a plane with the head, and is simply notched. The barb piece of bone is 8 inches long and is let into a socket in end of arrow shaft. It has a strong barb on one side at right angles to the head. It is ornamented with deep longitudinal furrows. The triangular head of bone is a flat blade inserted neatly in a deep slit at the head of the barb piece, which is smoothed down so as to present no impediment to the passage into the animal struck.

> Cat. No. 127627, U. S. N. M. Alaska. Collected by J. W. Johnson.

FIG. 2. SHAFT, of spruce, cylindrical; coarsely made; banded with red paint. Feathers, three, seized with sinew, one of them at the middle of the flat side and the other two at the round corners of the other side. As usual with the Eskimo, the end of these feathers is sunk into notches cut in the soft wood. The nock is flat; the notch, angular. There is a barb piece of bone set into the shaft, at the end, by a cylindrical tenon, and is seized with sinew. Blade, of iron, set into the barb piece at right angles to the plane of its longest diameter and cross section. One barb in the side of the barb piece. Total length, 28 inches.

> Cat. No. 127627, U. S. N. M. Eskimo, Bristol Bay, Alaska. Collected by J. W. Johnson.

FIG. 3. SHAFT, of cedar, cylindrical. Shaftment, flat, banded with blue stripes. Feathers, three, seized with sinew thread and standing off quite a distance from the shaftment. The nock is flat; notch, angular. Blade, of slate, inserted into the end of the barb piece of bone. The single barb is 1¼ inches long and is formed on one side by a narrow notch. Two shallow gutters extend from this barb to the end of the shaft. The barb piece is fitted into the end of the shaft by a dowel or peg made of bone and lashed with a fine sinew thread. The blade is covered by a cap made of two pieces of cedar neatly cut for the blade and the end of the barb piece and joined together with a braid of sinew. This is a very effective and neatly-made weapon. Total length of shaft, 30 inches.

> Cat. No. 90404, U. S. N. M. Kadiak, Alaska. Collected by Wm. J. Fisher.

FIG. 4. SHAFT, of cedar; about half an inch in diameter in the middle, tapering slightly forward to within two inches of the end, where it is cylindrical, and tapering backward gradually to the nock. Feathers, three, laid on at equal distances apart and seized with fine sinew thread. The plume of the feather is neatly cut into a triangular shape. The shaftment is painted red. The nock is a bulb of extraordinary size, which gives the hunter all the grip he could ask. Notch, shallow and angular. Foreshaft, of bone, let into the end of the shaft by a dowel cut on the end of the bone. A small wooden plug is inserted into the front end of this and perforated. The head is a small triangular piece of bone, barbed on one side, cut away at the butt to form a very short dowel to be inserted into the perforation in the shaftment, and perforated near the base to receive a lanyard or martingale of braided sinew, which, near the other extremity, has two branches, one of which is attached to the front of the shaft and the other towards the butt end. This arrow operates in the following manner: When this line is unrolled it resembles a kite's tail—the bird to which the barb is attached representing the tail and the spreading bifurcation the point attached to the kite. This line is neatly rolled up on the shaft to the end of the foreshaft. The barbed head is then put in place; the line tucked under the coil and drawn tight, but not fastened. The hunter shoots the game with this arrow; the barb penetrates beneath the skin; the sudden movement of the sea otter withdraws the barb head from the foreshaft and loosens the slight fastening of the coil, which is then unrolled, and the bone head, being heavier, sinks in the water, while the light shaft supports the feather above the surface, the whole apparatus acting as a drag to the game and also as a buoy to enable the hunter to follow. Total length of shaft, 34¼ inches.

Cat. No. 16407, U. S. N. M. Kadiak, Alaska. Collected by W. H. Dall.

Fig. 5. SHAFT, of spruce, cylindrical. Shaftment, flattened. Three black feathers, seized with sinew. The nock is flat; notch, rectangular. The barbed head is leaf-shaped, with two small barbs on one side and one on the other. The head is fitted into the end of the shaft, which is seized with sinew. Length, 33½ inches.

Cat. No. 19382, U. S. N. M. Eskimo, Cook's Inlet, Alaska. Collected by Mr. Early.

Fig. 6. SHAFT, of spruce wood, cylindrical. Shaftment, flattened. Feathers, three, seized at one end with sinew and at the other with sinew thread. The feathers are laid on at the round corners of the flattened shaftment, so that really there could have been another feather at one of the corners. The nock is flat; the notch of the usual U shape. Foreshaft, of walrus ivory, one end cut into the shape of a tenon and inserted in the end of the shaft and seized with sinew thread. The front end of this shaft is perforated and into this is inserted a plug of soft wood. The delicate head has two barbs on either side, and a perforation through the body for holding a sinew cord, which attaches it to the shaft. The head is loosely fitted into the foreshaft by a conical tang. This weapon is shot from a bow into a sea otter or other game. The barbed head becomes fastened in the skin and withdraws from the foreshaft. The ivory head sinks in the water, leaving a feathered shaft bobbing in the air. The whole acts as a drag upon the game and also enables the hunter to follow. Length of shaft and foreshaft, 31¾ inches.

Cat. No. 72412, U. S. N. M. Eskimo, Bristol Bay. Collected by Charles McKay.

PLATE LII.

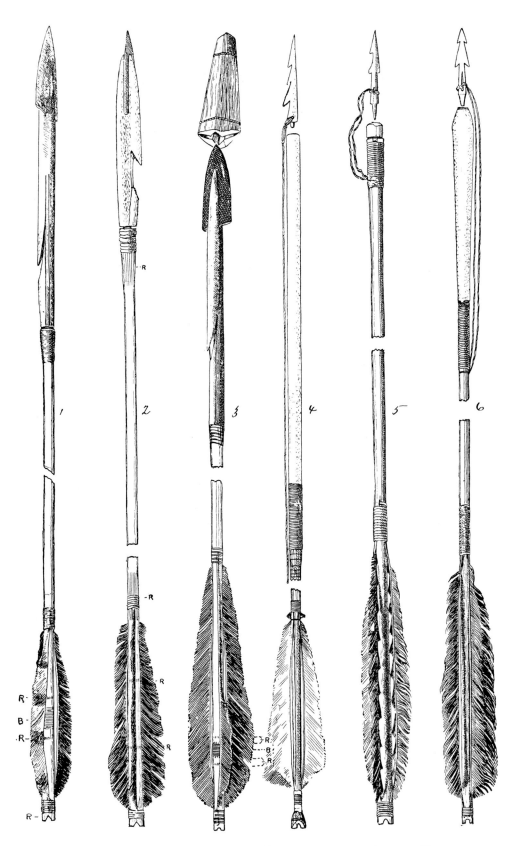

BARBED AND HARPOON ARROWS OF THE ESKIMO ABOUT THE ALASKAN PENINSULA.

EXPLANATION OF PLATE LIII.

ESKIMO ARROWS, WITH FLAT FEATHERS AND LONG POINTS.

FIG. 1. SHAFT, of spruce wood, tapering from the head backwards to a point, to which a single feather is fastened by a seizing of sinew. The point, of walrus ivory, inserted in a split in the end of the shaft, and seized with sinew. Other specimens of these darts are seized with a fine rawhide line of babiche. Length of shaft and point, 19 inches.

Cat. No. 45476, U. S. N. M. Eskimo, Cape Nome, Alaska. Collected by E. W. Nelson.

FIG. 3. SHAFT, of pine, short and thick. Head, of bone, spatulate and spliced on to the shaft and held in place by sinew. In the specimens of this type made after contact with the whites the type of this spatulate point has a saw cut across the end, into which a blade of iron is inserted and held in place by a rivet. The connection between these two forms should be especially noted, as the more recent could not be explained without comparison with the ancient form. Length of shaft, 1 foot 5½ inches; foreshaft, 5 inches.

Cat. Nos. 34052-55, U. S. N. M. Eskimo of Cumberland Gulf. Collected by Ludwig Kumlien.

FIG. 2. Similar to fig. 3, except that the head is of iron.

FIG. 4. SHAFT, of spruce wood. Head, a flat blade of iron, widened at the point and inserted into the split end of the shaft and held in place by the lashing of babiche or rawhide string. Feathers, two, laid on flat, the ends inserted into the wood of the shaft. Nock, flat; notch, large and deep.

Not numbered. St. Lawrence Island Eskimo. Collected by E. W. Nelson.

FIG. 5. SHAFT, of spruce wood, spliced, owing to the scarcity of material. Two feathers, laid on flat and seized with sinew. Nock, flat; notch, angular. The point, a bit of iron from a whaling ship, flattened out and fastened into a slit at the end of the shaft by a seizing of sinew thread. The point has been hammered and filed coarsely into cylindrical shape. Total length of shaft, 17 inches.

Cat. No. 30016, U. S. N. M. Collected by W. A. Münster.

PLATE LIII.

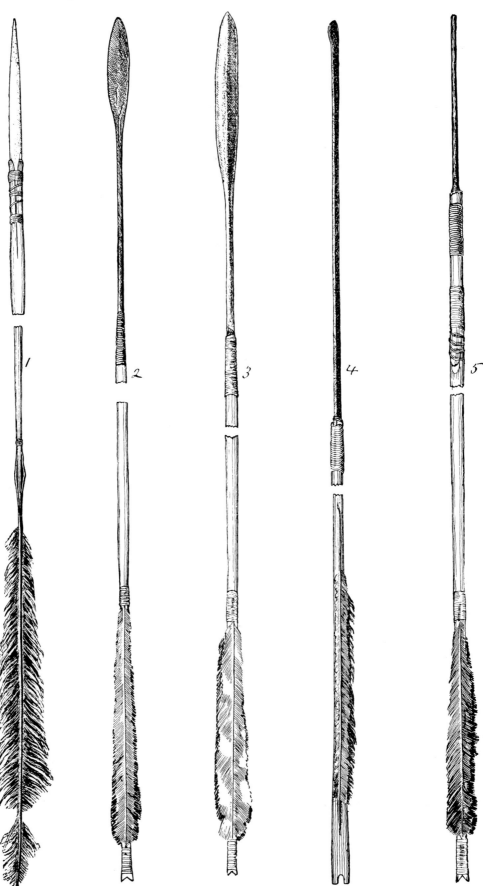

ESKIMO ARROWS WITH FLAT FEATHERS AND LONG POINTS.

BIRD BOLTS FROM VARIOUS AREAS.

FIG. 1. SHAFT, cylindrical and flattened toward the notch. No feathers. Notch, with parallel sides. Head, a bullet-shaped piece of walrus ivory, perforated and fitted on the end of the shaft. Total length of shaft, 25 inches.

Not numbered, U. S. N. M. St. Lawrence Islands. Collected by E. W. Nelson.

FIG. 2. THE SHAFT, cylindrical and flattened toward the nock. Feathers, two, on inner ends, securely inserted into gashes on the side of the shaft, and the outer extremity seized with sinew. Notch, shallow. Head, of bone or antler, blunt-shaped, like a flower bud, with seven nodes or projections around the margin. This style of arrow is very common in this region. The head is found in a great variety of shapes, but they are all used for the purpose of stunning birds without drawing blood. Total length, 27 inches.

Cat. No. 45432, U. S. N. M. Eskimo, Cape Darby, Alaska. Collected by E. W. Nelson.

FIG. 3. SHAFT, of cedar; 25 inches long; narrow streak of red ocher around at upper extremity. Shaftment, flat; feather end near the nock without seizing; at the other extremity seized with sinew thread. Nock, flat; notch, very deep. The head is a cylinder of antler, hollowed at the lower extremity and fitted into the shaft with a conical tenon fitted into a cavity of the same shape. The head, at its upper extremity, is gashed, so as to have four pointed projections.

Cat. No. 33833, U. S. N. M. Eskimos of Pastolik. Collected by E. W. Nelson.

FIG. 4. SHAFT, a piece of hard wood, cut down so as to leave the tip of the shaft and the nock wide spreading. Feathers, three, long, fastened to the shaft by wide strips of sinew. No ornamentation, but very carefully made. Length, 27 inches.

Cat. No. 23736, U. S. N. M. Indians of Devil's Lake. Collected by Paul Beckwith.

FIG. 5. The whole arrow is of a single piece, without feathers. The head is a double pyramid. The nock is much expanding; the notch, shallow. In the companion arrow to this one the head is a double cone. Total length of shaft, 24½ inches.

Cat. Nos. 8509 and 8508, U. S. N. M. Shoshones. Collected by Mr. Waters.

PLATE LIV.

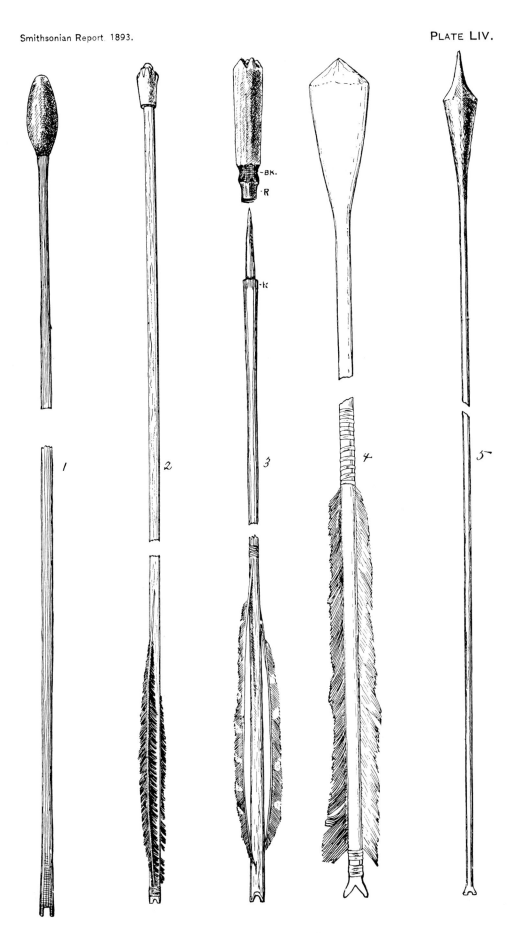

BIRD BOLTS FROM VARIOUS AREAS.

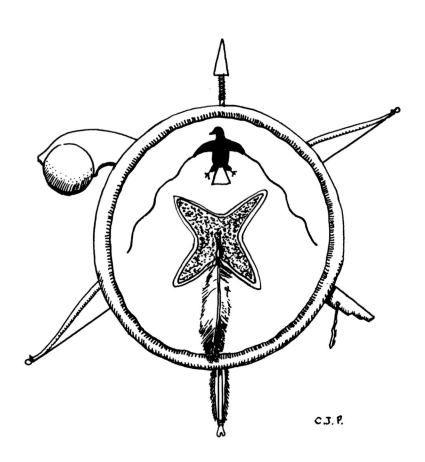

EXPLANATION OF PLATE LV.

WESTERN ESKIMO BARBED ARROWS.

FIG. 1. THE SHAFT tapers both ways from the middle and is flattened at the nock. Feathers, two, laid on spirally and seized at the end with sinew. Nock, flat; notch, U-shaped. The blade of the head is sagittate, and there are two barbs on each side of the tang, which is inserted in the end of the shaft and seized with sinew. Length, 29 inches.

> Cat. No. 72765, U. S. N. M.; also 72759. Ooglaamie Eskimo, Point Barrow. Collected by Capt. P. H. Ray, U. S. Army.

There is a great variety of form in this class of arrows, the design being always the same. In one specimen the tang is cylindrical and a series of barbs is filed on the edges of the blade. In another the tang is made of walrus ivory, and the iron blade inserted into the end of this tang has barbs on the lower edges of the blade. In another specimen one-half of a pair of scissors is used as a head. The part in front of the hinge, filed with two edges, forms the blade, and the part behind the hinge is filed and straightened out so as to form the tang and a very efficient barb. This is a remarkable specimen of the adaptive genius of this people. In the shaping and filing of this scissors blade all of the characteristics and marks of the barbed arrow with a stone head are preserved, except that the metal is substituted for the bone and stone.

FIG. 2. SHAFT, of spruce wood, cylindrical. Shaftment, gradually flattened toward the nock. Feathers, two, extending off from the shaft, and seized with sinew-twisted thread. The nock is flattened; notch, parallel-sided. The barb, a piece of antler, sharpened at one end, inserted into the end of the shaft, and seized with fine sinew thread. The four barbs are on one side of the barb piece, and they project from the shaft, as in a feather, and this effect is emphasized by a little furrow just where the barbs proceed from the shaft. The point, a formidable blade of iron, with jagged barbs at the lower extremities, inserted into a "saw cut" on the end of the barb piece and fastened with a copper rivet.

> Cat. No. A and B. 43352, U. S. N. M. Eskimo, Upper Yukon. Collected by E. W. Nelson.

FIG. 3. SHAFT, of spruce, cylindrical, flattened towards the end. Feathers, two, seized with sinew twine. Nock, flat; notch, U-shaped. The head is in two parts. The shank is barbed on one side, inserted into the end of the shaft, and seized with twisted sinew. The head is sagittate; the tang inserted into a cut in the end of the shank and seized with sinew. Total length of shaft, 29½ inches.

FIG. 4. Similar to fig. 3, excepting that the head is all of iron. The long shank is serrated on the edges and the leaf-shaped blade has also barbs near the base. Length, 25¾ inches.

> Cat. No. 875, U. S. N. M. Mackenzie River. Collected by R. W. MacFarlane.

FIG. 5. SHAFT, of spruce, cylindrical. Shaftment, flat. Feathers, two, seized at the end with twisted sinew, standing off from the shaftment. The nock is flat and seized with twisted sinew; notch, U-shaped. The head is a piece of sheet iron inserted into a cut in the end of the shaft and seized with twisted sinew. Three abnormally large barbs on each side of the head. Length, 30 inches.

> Cat. No. 1966, U. S. N. M. Mackenzie River. Collected by R. W. MacFarlane.

Fig. 6. Shaft of spruce. The head is of steel or iron. On each side of the head are six sharp barbs put in with a file, and a portion of the long tang protruding from the shaft is also serrated. The head is split, the tang driven in and held in place by a lashing of sinew twine. Feathers, two, seized at the end by narrow bands of sinew cord and standing off from the shaft. This type of arrow is evidently the direct descendant of the aboriginal form, in which the head consists of a barbed piece and the blade. These murderous heads of iron exist in great variety over the Mackenzie region and have evidently been procured by the Eskimo from the Hudson Bay Company. A collection of them is a very interesting study in the variation of the arrowhead. Length of shaft, 2 feet; foreshaft, 5 inches.

Cat. No. 875, U. S. N. M. Mackenzie River Eskimo. Collected by R. Kennicott.

Note.—Specimens exist in the National Museum in which the iron blade is attached to the bone barbed piece thus, and also specimens in which the blade is of bone. Thus connection between the three types is established.

PLATE LV.

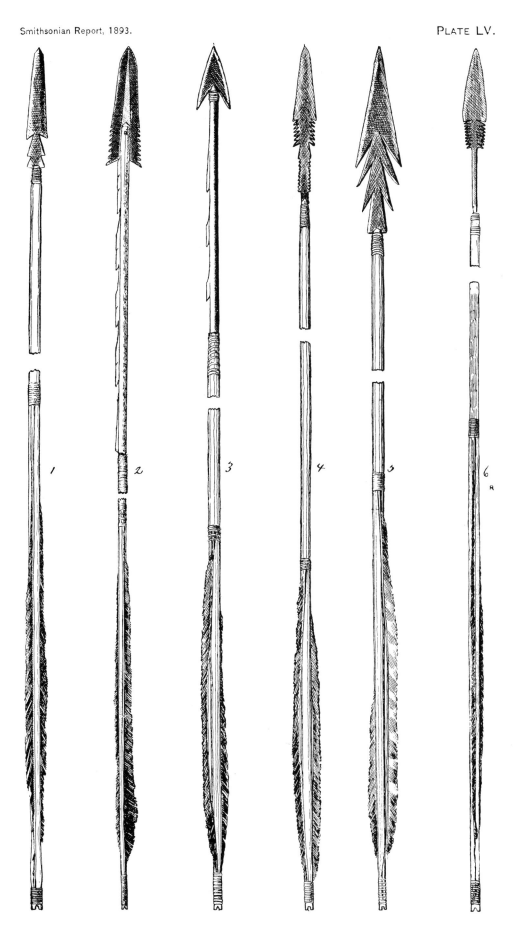

WESTERN ESKIMO BARBED ARROWS.

FIG. 1. SHAFT, of spruce wood, cylindrical. Shaftment flat. Feathers, two, seized with sinew. The nock is flat; the notch, U-shaped. The head is a triangular piece of ivory driven into the end of the shaft, and is seized with sinew. The point is formed by shaving off the sides of the pyramid. Total length, 25 inches.

> Cat. No. 89904, U. S. N. M. Eskimo of Point Barrow, Alaska. Collected by Lieut. Ray, U. S. Army.

FIGS. 2, 3, 4. SHAFT, of spruce, the head is a piece of bone sharpened at the point, and on the sides are cut barbs, which vary in number among different examples. The head is set very loosely into a socket in the end of the shaft by means of a tapering dowel, the object being to leave the head to rankle in the deer or other animal killed. There is a great variety of these rankling arrows in the collection of the National Museum. Length of shaft, 2 feet 11 inches; foreshaft, 8 inches.

> Cat. No. 2674, U. S. N. M. Eskimo of Fort Anderson River. Collected by G. R. McFarlane.

FIG. 5. SHAFT, cylindrical. Shaftment, flattened transversely to the plane of the arrowhead. Feathers, three, laid on flat and seized with twisted sinew. Notch, angular. The head of this arrow consists of two parts—the barb piece and the point. The barb piece is of bone or antler pointed and inserted into the end of the shaft and seized with sinew. Barbs, two, standing out from one side. The arrowhead, of chert, neatly chipped, hastate-shaped, inserted into a slit in the end of the barb piece and seized with sinew, which is laid on in a groove. These points are very easily drawn out. Other specimens from this same quiver vary in size of the barb piece and the length and serrations of the chipped blade. Total length of shaft, 30 inches.

> Cat. No. 72785, U. S. N. M. Eskimo of Point Barrow. Collected by Capt. Ray, U. S. Army.

FIG. 6. SHAFT, of spruce. Feathers, two, loosely laid on and fastened with sinew. Head, one blade of a pair of scissors driven into the shaft and seized with rawhide. Length of shaft, 25 inches; foreshaft, 5 inches.

> Cat. No. 72757, U. S. N. M. Eskimo of Point Barrow. Collected by P. H. Ray, U. S. Army.

PLATE LVI.

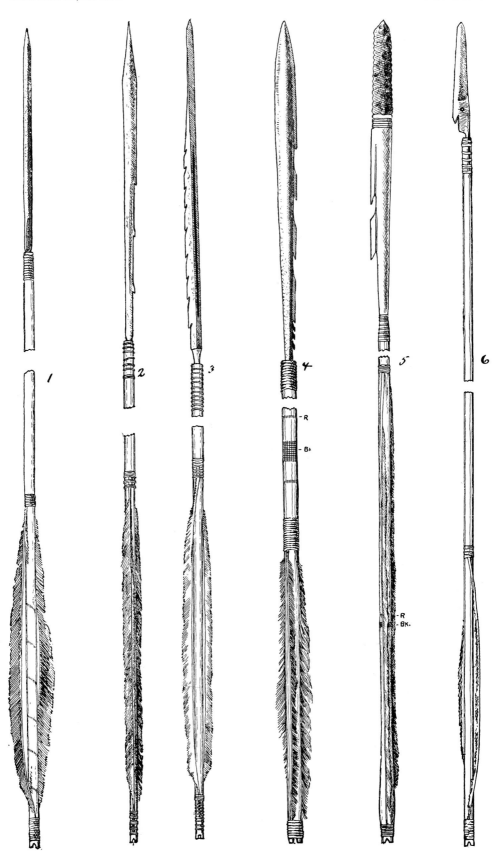

NORTHWESTERN ESKIMO RANKLING ARROWS.

EXPLANATION OF PLATE LVII.

BIRD BOLTS OF NORTHWESTERN ESKIMO.

FIG. 1. SHAFT, of wood, and the head, of bone, or ivory, or antler, is set on like the head of a cane and rounded. In one of the examples the end of the shaft is split and the head is held in by a wedge-shaped dowel. Bird arrow. Length, about 21 inches.

> Cat. Nos. 24579–80, U. S. N. M. Eskimo, St. Michaels, Alaska. Collected by Lucien Turner.

NOTE.—There is a great variety of these bird arrows used for the purpose of stunning water fowl. The shaft is a simple rod of different material, and the head is held on in various ways and seized with sinew.

FIG. 2. SHAFT, cylindrical. Shaftment, flattened. Feathers, three, held on with twisted sinew. Nock, flat; notch, U-shaped. The head is in the conventional form of the Eskimo bird arrowheads, fitted on to the wedge-shaped end of the shaft and seized with sinew. Length, 27 inches.

> Cat. No. 72772, U. S. N. M. Point Barrow. Collected by Capt. P. H. Ray, U. S. Army.

FIGS. 3, 5. SHAFT, of spruce, cylindrical. Shaftment, flattened at the end. Feathers, three, seized with twisted sinew. Nock, flat; notch, angular. Head, of iron, in imitation of the standard Eskimo bird arrow, the head of which is a club-shaped piece of ivory or bone with notches cut in the end so as to give the shape of a cross in section. This is designed to wound the bird and bring him down without shedding his blood.

FIG. 4. Precisely similar to fig. 3, excepting that the head is of ivory, and there are only two feathers. Length of both arrows, 27 inches.

> Cat. No. 1106, U. S. N. M. Eskimo, Mackenzie River. Collected by R. MacFarlane.

NOTE.—In some samples under this number the ivory or bone heads are ornamented with lines cut in. The shaft of the arrow is cut wedge-shaped, inserted into the long notch at the base of the head, and nicely seized with sinew, which is laid on in a groove or countersink cut into the base of the bone head. The workmanship of this arrow is excellent.

PLATE LVII.

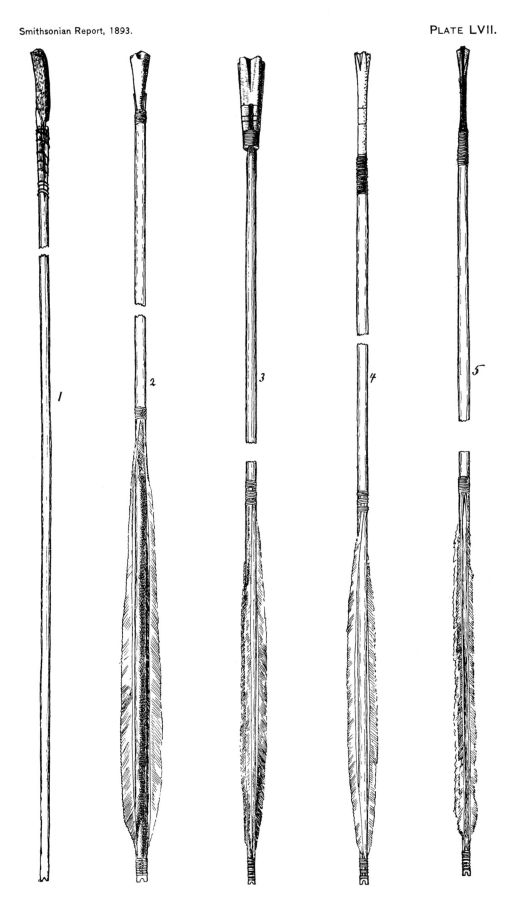

BIRD BOLTS OF NORTHWESTERN ESKIMO.

EXPLANATION OF PLATE LVIII.

COMPOUND ESKIMO ARROWS, WITH TWO FEATHERS, OR NONE, AND FLAT NOCKS.

FIG. 1. SHAFT, cylindrical. No feathers. Nock, flat; notch, large and U-shaped. The head consists of a long shank of bone, in the end of which an iron blade is inserted and held in place by an iron rivet. The arrow shaft is cut wedge-shaped and fitted into an angular notch in the bone shank, held in place by wooden rivets, and seized with sinew. Total length, 26½ inches.

FIG. 3 is similar to fig. 1.

> Cat. No 2529, U. S. N M. Asiatic Eskimo. Collected by Commodore Rodgers, U. S. Navy.

FIG. 2. SHAFT, short and rudely made. Head is in two parts; the long shank of iron, on the outer end of which a blade of iron is riveted. Feathers, two, laid on flat and held in place by sinew. All of the specimens from this region are very poor, owing to the lack of wood, and they are also much modified by contact with the whites (thanks to the early appearance in this region of whale ships). Compare fig. 4. Length, shaft, 2 feet 2 inches; foreshaft, 6 inches.

> Cat. No. 30016, U. S. N M. Eskimo of Cumberland Gulf. Collected by W. A. Münster, U. S. Navy.

FIG. 4. THE SHAFT is of pine. The head consists of two parts, a shank of bone and a blade of iron let into the saw cut and riveted in place. The shank is spliced onto the shaft and seized with sinew twine. Feathers, two, laid on flat and held in place by a rough wrapping of sinew. Nock, flat. In this same number are other specimens differing from the one described in minute particulars. One specimen has a common nail for the head, with a piece of nail let in transversely as a stop. Other examples are unfinished. Length of shaft, 2 feet 1 inch.

> Cat. No. 90138, U. S. N. M. Whale River Indians, Eskimo stock, Labrador. Collected by Lucien Turner.

FIG. 5. The type is fully described and figured in Pl. LIX.

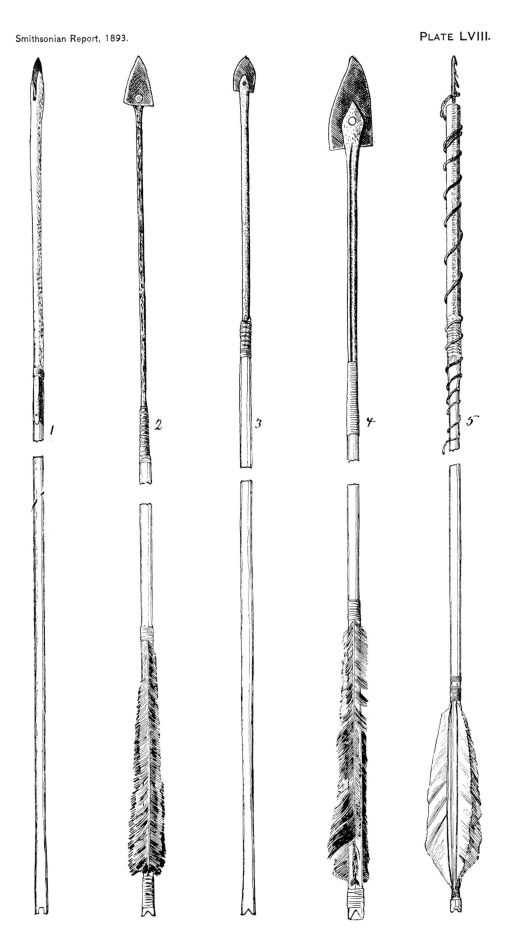

COMPOUND ESKIMO ARROWS, WITH TWO FEATHERS OR NONE AND FLAT NOCKS.

EXPLANATION OF PLATE LIX.

THE DISSECTION OF A SEA-OTTER ARROW, COOK'S INLET.

This is the most elaborate and ingenious arrow known, and all of its parts, in every specimen, are most delicately finished. Such a weapon may well have been used in hunting the most costly of fur-bearing animals—the otter.

The shaft is of spruce, gently tapering toward the nock, which is large and bell shape. Into the end of this shaft is inserted a foreshaft of bone, and into the end of this fits the barb. Feathers, three, symmetrically trimmed and seized at both ends with delicately-twisted sinew thread. The barbed head is perforated, and through these perforations is attached a braided line at least ten feet long. The other end of the line is attached to two points on the shaft by a martingale. When not in use, the line is coiled neatly on the shaft and the barb is put in place in the foreshaft. When the arrow is shot, the barb enters the flesh of the otter, the loose fastening is undone, the line unrolled, the foreshaft drops into the arrow; the shaft acts as a drag and the feathers as a buoy to aid the hunter in tracing the animal. See fig. 4., Pl. LII.

FIG. 1. Arrow with line unrolled showing relation of parts.

FIG. 2. The shaftment. Attention is drawn to the delicate seizing with sinew thread, the natty trimming of the feather, the most efficient nock.

FIG. 3. The lines and knots. Notice is given of the elegance of the braid, the efficient manner of " doing up" the line, the peculiar knot for the martingale.

FIG. 4. The arrow ready to be shot.

This form of arrow with its southern type of sinew-backed bow is found also on the Keniles, where these were taken by Alents, carried over by the Russians to hunt sea otter.

PLATE LIX.

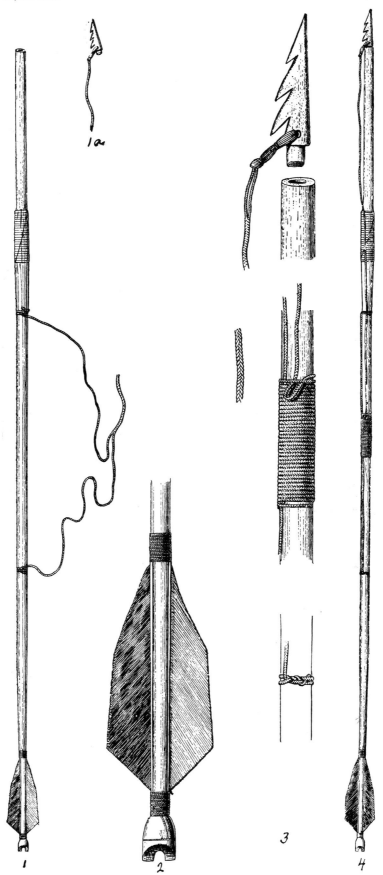

THE DISSECTION OF A SEA OTTER ARROW, COOK'S INLET.

C.J. Pugliese

EXPLANATION OF PLATE LX.

ARROWS WITH STOPS, RETRIEVING BARBS, OR COMPOUND PILE.

FIG. 1. Made of pine wood; the shaft, head, and point cut out of one piece. Feathers, three, 4¼ inches long, laid on flat in the following manner: The three feathers were first attached to the butt of the arrow by a coiled wrapping of sinew, their other extremities pointed backward; then they were doubled backward and the ends seized with sinew. This makes a very secure fastening for the feather. The coiled wrapping is continued over the nock and fastened off in the notch. Nock, flat; notch, U-shaped. The head, bulbous. The point is cut out of this by whittling away the wood so as to leave a long projection like a nail or spike. Total length, 31½ inches.

Cat. No. 90123, U. S. N. M. Eskimo, Ungava. Collected by L. M. Turner.

FIG. 2. Very rudely made. Shaft, of spruce. Shaftment, flat. Feathers, two, laid on flat, seized with sinew. The nock is flat and the notch angular. Head, a common cut nail, driven into the end of the shaft and seized with sinew. At the inner part of this seizing a piece of nail is lashed on crosswise so as to prevent the arrow going more than two inches into the body of the the game. Total length of shaft, 25 inches.

Cat. No. 90138, U. S. N. M. Whale River, Hudson Bay. Collected by Lucien Turner.

FIG. 3. THE SHAFT, of osier. There is no feather. The nock is tightly seized with sinew cord; notch, U-shaped. The peculiarity of this arrow is that the point, of iron or bone, is lashed to the beveled end of the shaft and the tang is projected backwards into a long barb. This arrow is used in shooting prairie dogs. It is said that the Navahoe uses now a little bit of mirror with which to throw the sunlight into the eyes of the prairie dog until he can get near enough to drive one of these arrows into his body. Upon the least alarm or injury the creatures dive into their holes and this arrow enables the hunter, if he strikes one of them, to retrieve his game. The action of this arrow is very similar to that of the vermin hook used by the Ute Indians, and also to those of the northwest coast. Total length of shaft, 33 inches (32½ inches).

Cat. No. 126740, U. S. N. M. Navahoe Indians. Collected by Thomas Keam.

FIG. 4. THE SHAFT is of spruce wood, ornamented here and there with band of red paint, cylindrical. Shaftment, flat. Feathers, three, seized at their ends with twisted sinew thread. One feather is in the middle of one of the flat sides; the other two feathers are at the round corners of the other side. The flat nock flares a little upward, and the notch is angular. This is a bident or double-pointed arrow, having two barbs of bone inserted into the end of the shaft, so as to give them a spread of three-fourths of an inch at their points, one of which is a little longer than the other. They are held to the shaft by a wrapping of sinew cord. The barbs face inward. Total length of shaft, 26 inches.

Cat. No. 76705, U. S. N. M. Eskimo, Bristol Bay; Fort Alexandra, Alaska. Collected by J. W. Johnson.

FIG. 5. SHAFT, of spruce, painted red. Feathers, three, roughly seized with sinew. Nock, flat; notch, U-shaped. The three barbs of the trident are inserted in the end of the shaft so as to be about an inch apart at the outer point. The barbs, of bone, are serrated on the inside. They are held in place by a wrapping of sinew cord at their lower extremities, a curious braid of the same cord attaching them to the tip of the shaft and holding them in place. Length of shaft, 35 inches.

Cat. No. 72413, U. S. N. M. Southern Alaska. Collected by Charles McKay.

FIG. 6. SHAFT, of spruce wood. The lower end has been broken off. The upper portion of this weapon deserves especial study. A little band of ivory, fitted over the shaft, $1\frac{1}{2}$ inches from the upper end. Precisely similar bands are frequently labeled ornaments. Into the extremity of the shaft is inserted a delicate point of walrus ivory, triangular in cross section. Two of the edges are finely barbed. Three larger barbs, also triangular in section, have their lower ends driven into the shaft under the ivory band, and the edges lie along in grooves extending to the end of the shaft. The barbs of these three points are on the inside. Just at the end of the shaft each of these outer barbs is perforated, and sinew thread attaches them together and also to the central barb, and is also wrapped around the bases of these barbs just above the ivory band. Length of outer barbs, 6 inches.

This arrow represents a type Cat. No. 48342, U. S. N. M. Nunivak Island. Collected by E. W. Nelson.

PLATE LX.

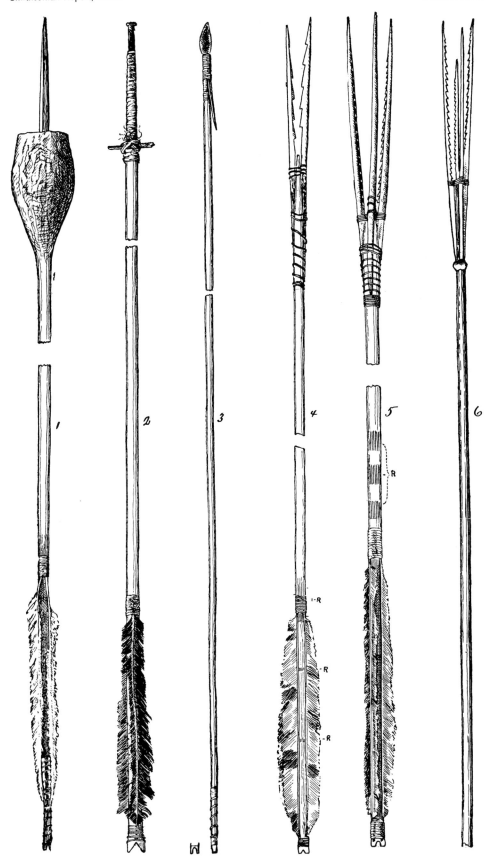

ARROWS WITH STOPS, RETRIEVING BARBS, OR COMPOUND PILE.

PLAIN BOWS FROM THE SOUTHWEST, AND SINEW-LINED, NARROW TYPE.

FIG. 1. Bow, of hard wood, rudely whittled out of a pole, showing bark and knots on the back. Length, 4 feet 6 inches. Notice that bows equally rude are found at Tierra del Fuego.

> Cat. No. 1976, U. S. N. M. Dieguenos Indians, San Diego, California. Collected by Dr. Edward Palmer.

FIG. 2. Bow, of mesquit wood. Rectangular in cross section, tapering from the grip; single curve. Bow string of two-ply sinew cord. Length, 3 feet 6 inches.

> Cat. No. 126643, U. S. N. M. Tarahumara, Chihuahua, Mexico. Collected by Dr. Edward Palmer.

FIG. 3. Bow, of cotton wood, cut out of a rod leaving the back untrimmed; single curve. Bow string of sinew cord, two-ply. Length, 4 feet 6 inches.

> Cat. No. 76021, U. S. N. M. Pima Indians, Arizona. Collected by Dr. Palmer.

It should be remarked that these plain bows with rounded and rectangular cross section represent the whole area southward to Cape Horn.

FIG. 4. SINEW-LINED BOW made of hard wood. Back lined with sinew and laid on with glue; reenforced by fifteen transverse bands of sinew. The grip wrapped with buckskin string. The bow string of sinew cord, two-ply. Length, 3 feet 8 inches.

> Cat. No. 75156, U. S. N. M. Navajo Indians, New Mexico. Collected by Bureau of Ethnology.

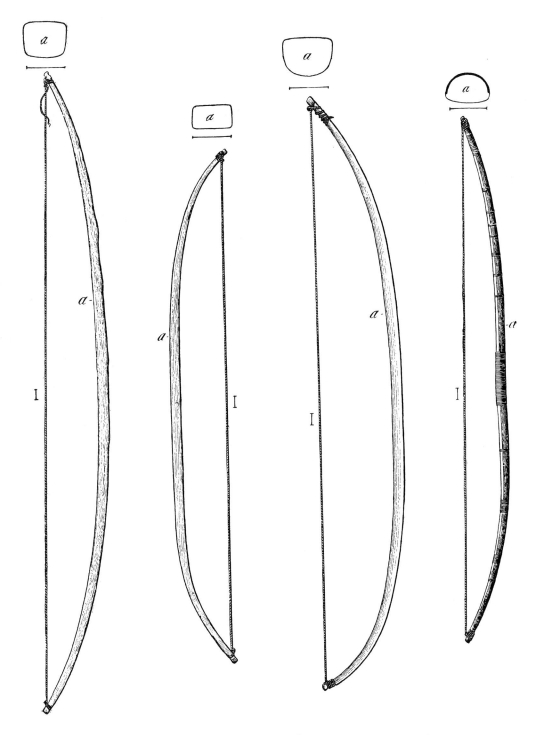

PLAIN BOWS FROM THE SOUTHWEST, AND SINEW-LINED BOW, NARROW TYPE.

EXPLANATION OF PLATE LXII.

Plain, Sinew-lined, and Compound Bows, the last named also Sinew-lined.

FIG. 1. Bow of hard wood, ovoid in section, single curve; string of sinew cord. Length, 4 feet 1 inch.

> Cat. No. 130616, U. S. N. M. Crow Indians, Montana. Collected by Maj. C. S. Bendire, U. S. Army.

FIG. 2. Bow, made of hickory, with a double curve—the lower curve larger than the other. The back neatly lined with sinew, and the ends wrapped for two or three inches with shredded sinew. Grip bound with buckskin string. Bowstring, three-ply sinew cord, back painted white. Length, 3 feet 5 inches.

> Cat. No. 8418, U. S. N. M. Gros Ventres, Dakota. Collected by Dr. Washington Mathews, U. S. Amry.

FIG. 3. COMPOUND BOW, made of two sections of cow's horn, spliced together in the middle and held by three rivets. Lined on the back with sinew, which covers also the nocks. Curved in shape of Cupid's bow, bound at the grip and the curve of the limbs with bands of red flannel, which is held in place by seizings of buckskin string wrapped here and there with broad quill, dyed yellow. The horns are also wrapped with shredded sinew. Bowstring, a three-ply sinew cord End of the bow ornamented with tufts of horsehair and fur. Length, 3 feet.

> Cat. No. 154015, U. S. N. M. Sioux Indians, Montana. Collected by Gen. Hazen, U. S. Army.

Special attention is called to the union of the compound and sinew lined bow in one specimen.

FIG. 4. Similar to No. 3, but was collected long ago from the Gros Ventres, Upper Missouri, by Dr. Washington Mathews, who spent a number of years among these people. Contact with the Great Interior Basin is shown by the union of the compound bow and the Shoshonean type of sinew-lined bow. Length, 36 inches.

PLATE LXII.

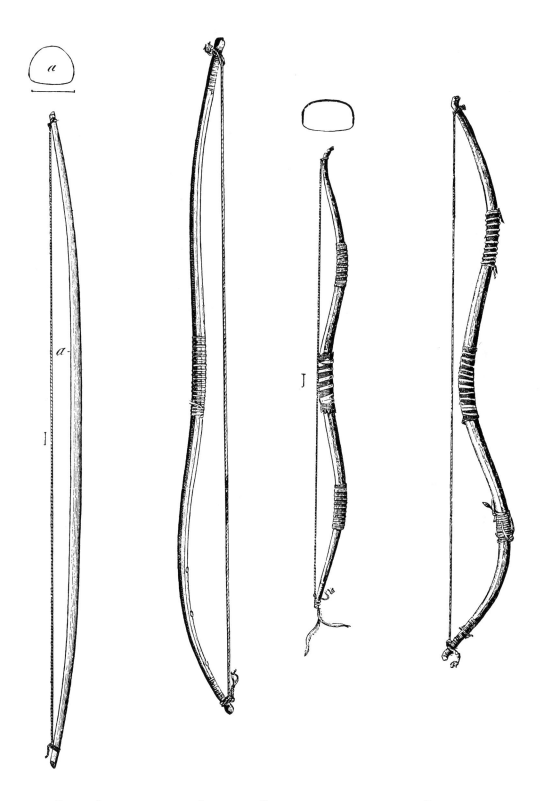

PLAIN, SINEW-LINED, AND COMPOUND BOWS, THE LAST NAMED ALSO SINEW-LINED.

EXPLANATION OF PLATE LXIII.

SINEW-LINED BOWS, BROAD TYPE. ONE BOW PLAIN.

FIG. 1. Bow, made of yew. This is a bow with a single curve on the back, double curve on the inside, broad and flat. Constricted at the grip and narrowing toward the nocks. Along the inside is a little furrow. The grip is ornamented with a tuft of long hair seized in place by a band of birch bark. This bow is exactly of the form of the sinew-lined bows farther south and inland. Perhaps the cold and dampness of the coast regions are unfavorable, affecting the glue. The bowstring is a single ribbon of sinew twist. Length, 3 feet 10 inches.

> Cat. No. 72656, U. S. N. M. Makah Indians, Cape Flattery. Collected by J. G. Swan.

FIG. 2. Bow, made of yew and lined along the back with sinew, shredded and mixed with glue, which is wrapped around the horns of the bow and molded to form the nocks. Single curve, excepting at the ends where the limbs turn gracefully backward. The grip and horns are wrapped with buckskin string. Bowstring, sinew cord, three-ply. Length, 3 feet 5 inches.

> Cat. No. 2058, U. S. N. M. Tejon Indians, California. Collected by John Xantbus.

FIG. 3. Bow, made of yew wood. Broad and thin at the grip, tapering in width and thickness toward the nocks, which are turned outward. The back of the bow is lined with shredded sinew, laid on closely like the bark on a tree, and painted green and decorated with tufts of otter skin and strips of dressed hide, seized with sinew. The grip is covered with a seizing of buckskin string. The horns of the bow turn outward. The bowstring is made of twisted sinew. Length, 3 feet 10 inches.

> Cat. No. 19322, U. S. N. M. McCloud River Indians, Copehan stock, California. Collected by Livingston Stone.

FIG. 4. SINEW-LINED BOW, made of yew. Broad and flat, lined on the back with sinew laid on in glue and ornamented with figures painted green. Narrowed somewhat at the grip and bound with buckskin string. Around the horns buckskin is glued and bands of sinew wrapped and the nocks ornamented with tufts of fur. Bowstring is a loose twine of sinew cord. Length, 3 feet 8 inches.

> Cat. No. 131110, U. S. N. M. Pitt River Indians, Northern California. Collected by N. J. Purcell.

PLATE LXIII.

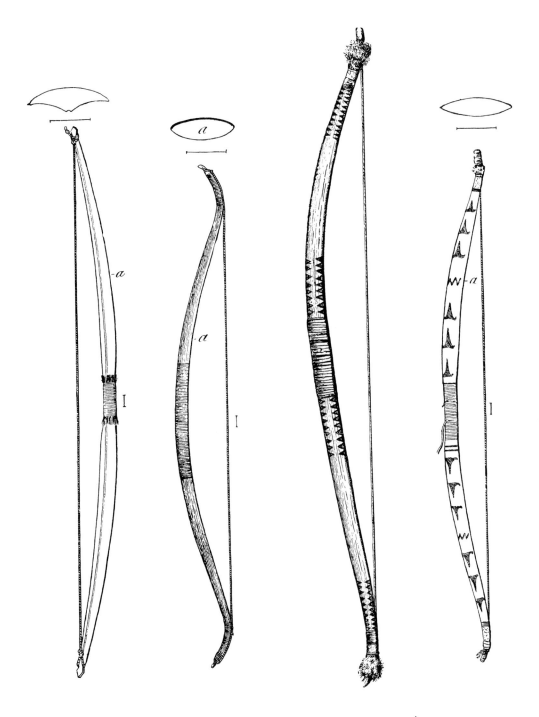

SINEW-LINED BOWS, BROAD TYPE. ONE BOW PLAIN.

EXPLANATION OF PLATE LXIV.

PLAIN BOWS. ONE EXAMPLE COMPOUND WITH SINEW CABLE BACKING.

FIG. 1. Bow, of hickory. Rectangular in cross-section. Double curve, tapering toward the ends. Bowstring of very thick three-ply sinew cord. Length, 4 feet.

> Cat. No. 129873, U.S.N.M. Arapaho Indians, Nebraska. Collected by H. M. Creel.

FIG. 2. Bow, of willow; oval in section, tapering toward the ends slightly, double curve. Chief characteristic is a piece of wood on the inside of the grip, fastened like the bridge of a violin, and held in place by a buckskin cord to catch the blow of the string in relaxing. The bowstring is a tough one of rawhide. Length, 4 feet 5 inches.

> Cat. No. 75455, U.S.N.M. Kutchin, Inland Alaska. Collected by J. J. McLean.

FIG. 3. Bow, of willow; similar to 75455. Evidently unfinished. It is a weak weapon, and the bowstring is made of cotton thread. Length, 4 feet 1 inch.

> Cat. No. 63552, U.S.N.M. Kutchin Indians, Inland Alaska. Collected by J. J. McLean.

FIG. 4. COMPOUND BOW, made of three pieces of bone. The foundation is the grip or middle piece, to which the limbs are spliced and riveted. The back of this bow is slightly reenforced by five double strands of braided sinew or sennit, passing along the back from nock to nock, and held in place by a cross wrapping at the middle of the grip. Bowstring is made of four strands of sennit. The ends of this string are attached to loops of rawhide, which pass over the nocks. Length, 2 feet 8 inches.

> Cat. No. 34055, U. S. N. M. Eskimo, Cumberland Gulf. Collected by Ludwig Kumlien.

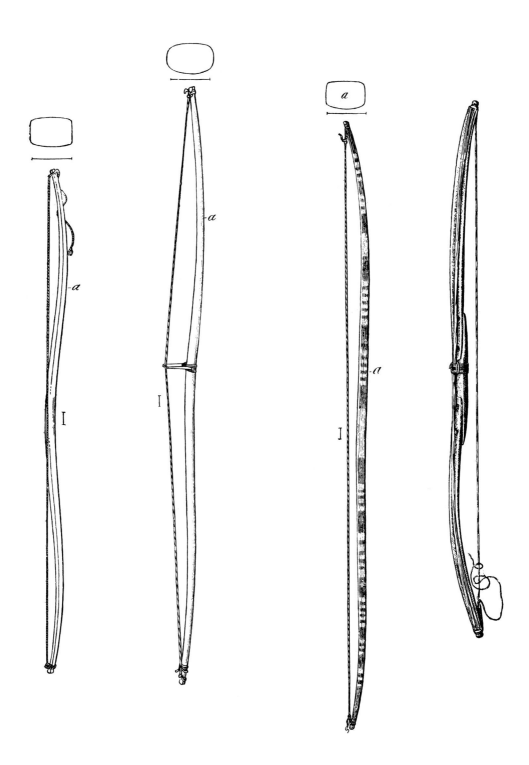

PLAIN BOWS. ONE EXAMPLE COMPOUND WITH SINEW CABLE BACKING.

EXPLANATION OF PLATE LXV.

SINEW-BACKED BOWS OF ESKIMO.

FIG. 1. Compound bow, made of reindeer antler and backed with sinew. The specimen is from Cumberland Gulf, the farthest point east at which sinew-backed bows have been found. This is an interesting specimen also because it exhibits the method of making the compound bow after the advent of the whalers. The grip piece is spliced and riveted to the limbs. In the old régime these three pieces were fastened together by lashings of sinew cord or braid, very strongly at the points where the upper and lower seizing occur in this bow. Two views given. Murdoch says of this type: "The main part of the reenforcement or backing consists of a continuous piece of stout twine made of sinew, generally a 3-strand braid, but sometimes a twisted cord, and often very long (sometimes 40 or 50 yards in length). One end of this is spliced or knotted into an eye, which is slipped round one 'nock' of the bow, usually the upper one. The strands then pass up and down the back and round the nocks. A comparatively short bow, having along its back some dozen or twenty such plain strands, and finished off by knotting the end about the 'handle,' appears to have been the original pattern. The bow from Cumberland Gulf (fig. 1) is such a one, in which the strands have been given two or three turns of twine from the middle. They are kept from untwisting by a 'stop' round the handle, which passes between and around the strands."

Cat. No. 34053, U. S. N. M. Collected by L. Kumlien.

FIG. 2. Southern type of sinew-backed bows of Murdoch. The essential features of these southern bows are—

First. The substitution of a columnar for a breaking strain upon the wood secured by winding a great many yards of sinew twine or braid backward and forward along the back of the bow, from nock to nock.

Second. The addition of strands in the cable inserted by means of half-hitches at various points, laid on as shown in the following plate.

Third. Holding the strands together in a cable by a coiled twine running from end to end.

Cat. No. 36032, U. S. N. M., Cape Romanzoff, collected by E. W. Nelson. Straight bow with the simplest form of southern backing.

PLATE LXV.

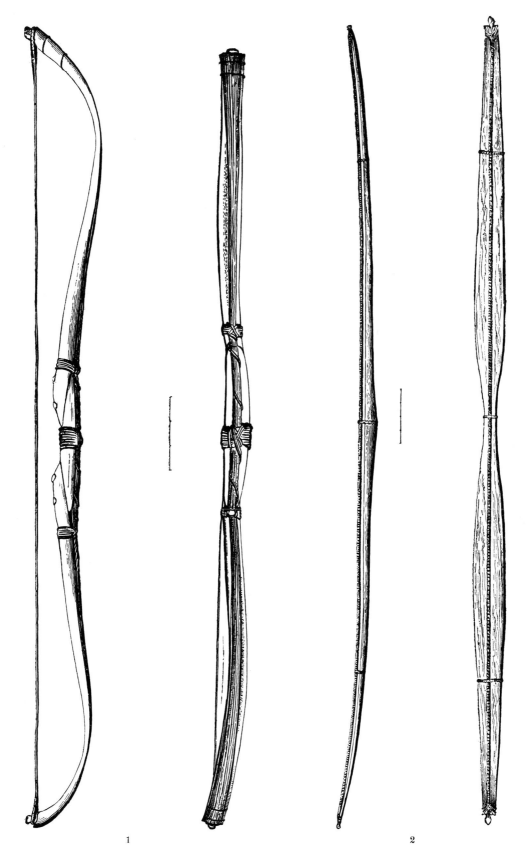

1   2

COMPOUND AND SINEW-BACKED BOWS OF ESKIMO.
(After Murdoch.)

EXPLANATION OF PLATE LXVI.

SINEW-BACKED BOWS OF ESKIMO. SOUTHERN TYPE.

FIG. 2*a*. One end of fig. 2 in the last plate, showing the form of the nock, the character of the braid of sinew, the method in which the cable is built up, the half hitches made about the bow, and the coil laid about the cable.

Cat. No. 36032, U. S. N. M. Eskimo of Cape Romanzoff. Collected by E. W. Nelson. (After Murdoch.)

FIG. 3. Straight bow, with Murdoch's southern type of backing. The peculiarity of this bow is shown in fig. 3*a*. After nearly all the filaments in the cable have been passed from nock to nock, the bowyer, stopped with his braid at a certain point, made two half hitches, and then added a strand to the cable by going to an equidistant point on the other side of the grip. This was repeated three times on this bow and the braid fastened off in the middle. The mark at the side of the bow denotes inches.

Cat. No. 72408, U. S. N. M. Bristol Bay. Collected by C. L. McKay.

PLATE LXVI.

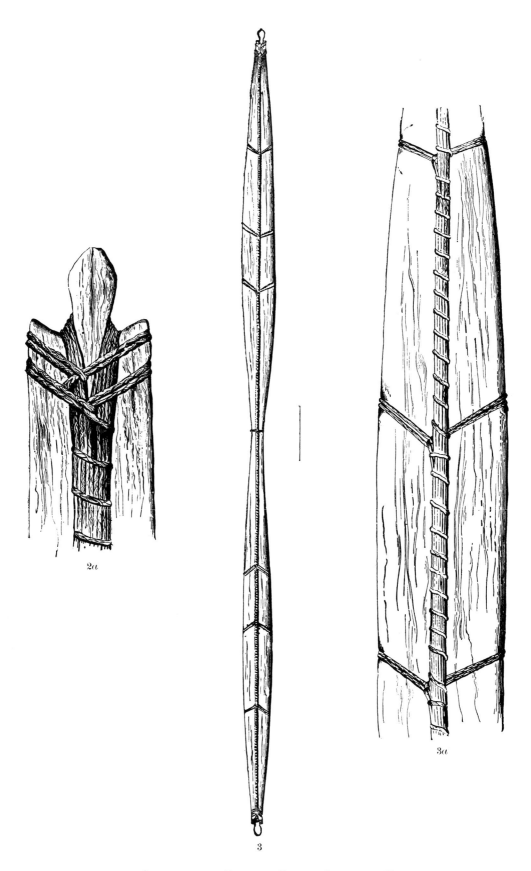

SINEW-BACKED BOWS OF ESKIMO, SOUTHERN TYPE.
(After Murdoch.)

EXPLANATION OF PLATE LXVII.

SINEW-BACKED BOWS OF ESKIMO.

PLATE LXVII represents four examples of sinew-backed bows of Murdoch's southern types. The following characteristics are to be noted: First, in all of them the backing extends from nock to nock with here and there extra strands let into the cable by means of any number of half hitches passing around the bow and into the cable. These have the additional value of keeping the wood from cracking. In the third example in the plate is exhibited the characteristics of the bent or Tatar pattern. The bow has really three curves, the great one in the middle and two shorter ones near the end. The bends where the small curves meet the larger one are strengthened with bridges of wood and seizing of sinew. In three specimens on the page the cable or backing has been twisted by means of an ivory lever described in the text and held thus by a seizing which is rove through one-half of the strands holding the whole in place. The twisting of the sinew serves to tighten the bow. In figures 4, 5, 7 the bow is shown with a device for keeping the cable from untwisting. In all examples except figure 6 one-half of the bow is shown.

In the order in which they appear upon the plate the bows are numbered Cat. No. 7972, U. S. N. M., from Bristol Bay, collected by Dr. Minor; No. 15651, Nuniviak Island, collected by W. H. Dall; No. 36028, Kuskoquim, collected by E. W. Nelson; No. 36034, collected by E. W. Nelson.

PLATE LXVII.

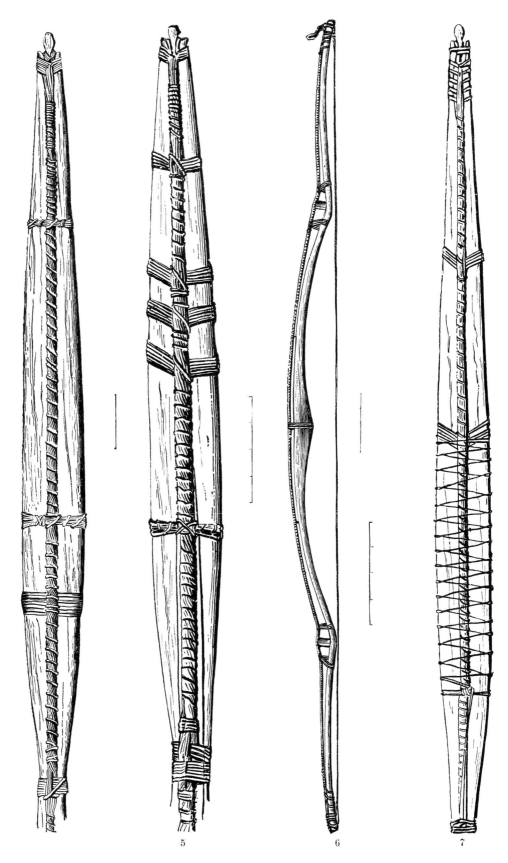

5   6   7

SINEW-BACKED BOWS OF ESKIMO, SOUTHERN TYPES.
(After Murdoch.)

SINEW-BACKED BOWS OF ESKIMO.

Plate showing Murdoch's Arctic type of bow. The noteworthy features are—

First. These bows are much shorter than those of southern type and are said by Murdoch to be of very graceful shape. In some examples the ends are bound up as in some of the southern bows and the back reenforced with a short rounded splint of wood or antler in the bend.

Second. The backing of these bows is always " of a very complicated and perfect pattern, usually very thoroughly incorporated with the bow by means of hitches and a very complete seizing of many turns running nearly the whole length of the bow and serving to equalize the distribution of the strain and thus prevent cracking."

Third. Another notable feature is in some examples the division of the backing into two cables in which the twist runs in opposite directions so that when the two cables are sewed together neither one can untwist. The examples shown in the plate are numbered as follows:

> *First.* Cat. No. 1972, U. S. N. M. Arctic bow from the Mackenzie region, back and side view. Collected by Ross.
>
> *Second.* Cat. No. 89245, U. S. N. M., from Point Barrow, collected by the U. S. International Polar Expedition. The wood is in shape of a Tatar bow. Figures 12 and 13 show the left-handed and right-handed "soldier's hitch."

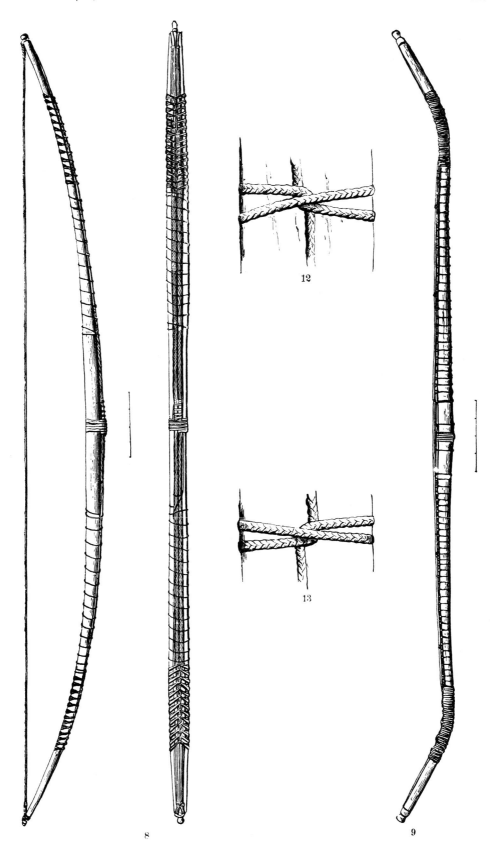

SINEW-BACKED BOWS OF ESKIMO, ARCTIC TYPES.
(After Murdoch.)

SINEW-BACKED BOWS OF ESKIMO, ARCTIC TYPES.

This plate exhibits the great variety of ways in which the sinew braid is administered upon the bow in the Arctic type for the purpose of minimizing the chances of breaking the very brittle wood of which they are made. The numbers upon the sides of the figures refer to descriptions by Murdoch, in the Report of the U. S. National Museum for 1884.

The first bow upon the plate, Fig. 10, is Cat. No. 89245, U. S. N. M., and the second figure is Cat. No. 72771, U. S. N. M., from Wainwright's Inlet. Collected by U. S. International Polar Expedition.

PLATE LXIX.

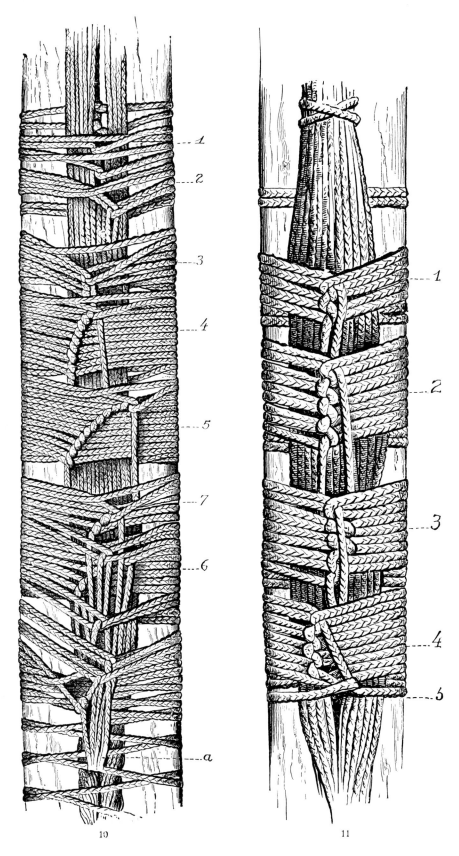

10

11

SINEW-BACKED BOWS OF ESKIMO, ARCTIC TYPE.
(After Murdoch.)

SINEW-BACKED BOWS OF ESKIMO, ARCTIC AND SOUTHERN TYPES.

Upon this plate are represented, first, a section of the Arctic bow to show the method in which short strands at the angles of the bow are administered in order to relieve the strain from the wood.

First figure shows section of Arctic bow 1970, U. S. N. M., from Mackenzie region, collected by B. R. Ross.

The other figure (15), showing back and side, is a bow of the southern type coming from the Yukon Delta and exhibits therefore some of the Arctic characteristics, such as the splint along the grip and the precautions against splitting.

Cat. No. 33867, U. S. N. M. Collected by E. W. Nelson on the delta of the Yukon River.

PLATE LXX.

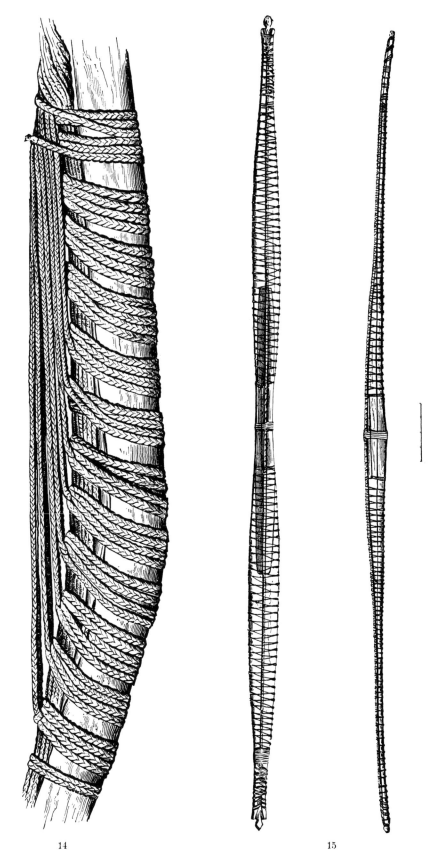

14

15

SINEW-BACKED BOWS OF ESKIMO, ARCTIC AND SOUTHERN TYPES.
(After Murdoch.)

EXPLANATION OF PLATE LXXI.

SINEW-BACKED BOWS OF ESKIMO.

The first two figures upon this plate, 16 and 17, illustrate a bow in which the southern type of wood has administered upon it the backing of the Arctic type. The method of administering the short strands by means of half hitches to prevent the splitting of the wood is exhibited in the second drawing, figure 17.

The last two figures upon this plate belong to what Murdoch calls the Western type. Perhaps it might be called the Chukchi type. The most noticeable feature is that the backing does not pass around the nocks at the ends of the bow, but the whole cable is held upon the back by means of a series of half hitches. The wood of the bow is either straight or of Tatar shape.

These examples are Cat. Nos. 8822, from Yukon Delta, figures 16 and 17, collected by W. H. Dall, and 2505 from Siberia, figure 18, collected by the North Pacific Exploring Expedition, U. S. N. M.

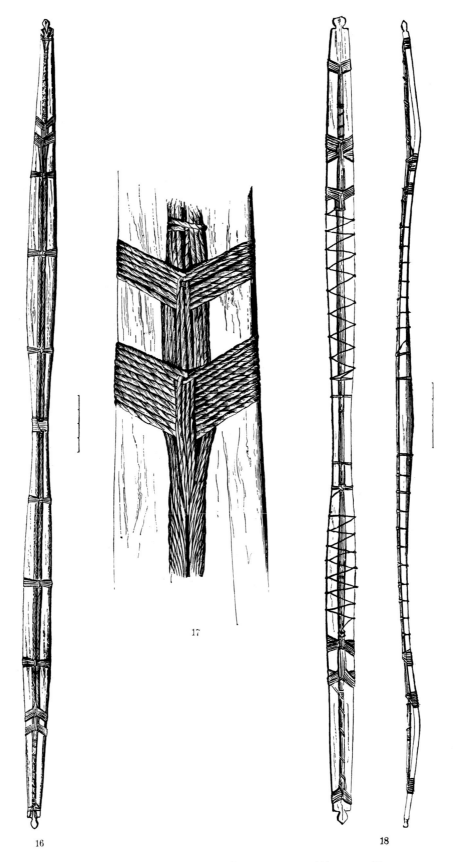

16

17

18

SINEW-BACKED BOWS OF ESKIMO, SOUTHERN AND WESTERN TYPE.
(After Murdoch.)

The peculiarities of the bow shown in the last plate and illustrated further on this plate are—

The extensions of their cables, one reaching nearly the whole length of the bow and attached close to the nocks, a second one further down upon the limbs, and a third one from the middle of the limbs. Between these two last-named points all the three cables are united into one passing across the grip.

This figure shows a portion of the first cable (the longest cable), the passing in strands of the second and third cables, and the union of all three into one. The second figure upon this plate (fig. 21) is a straight bow upon which the backing has upward of seventy strands twisted into three cables of Arctic type. In this example also, the longest cable passes around the nocks.

Section of Cat. No. 2505, U. S. N. M., and 2508, Eastern Siberia, collected by North Pacific Exploring Expedition.

19

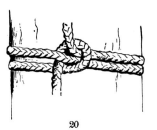

20

21

SINEW-BACKED BOWS OF ESKIMO, WESTERN TYPE.
(After Murdoch.)

EXPLANATION OF PLATE LXXIII.

SINEW-BACKED BOWS OF ESKIMOS, MIXED TYPES.

The first figure upon this plate exhibits the methods of seizing and the variety of attachments in passing the braided cord from the function of wrapping the bow on to the function of strand in the treble cable on the back. With a little patience it is easy to trace with the eye each braid strand from one function to the other.

The last two figures upon this plate represent a bow in which the backing is of the Arctic type and the shape of the bow approaches the Western type.

The first figure is Cat. No. 2505, U. S. N. M.

Second, Cat. No. 2506, E. Siberia. Collected by Northern Pacific Exploring Expedition.

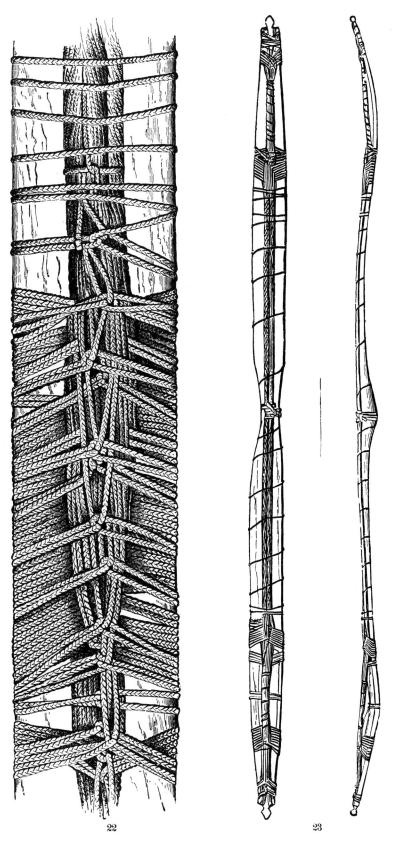

22   23

SINEW-BACKED BOWS OF ESKIMO, MIXED TYPES.
(After Murdoch.)

EXPLANATION OF PLATE LXXIV.

Sinew-Backed Bows of Eskimo.

The principal figure upon this plate shows the administration of the braided line just at the point where the third cable coming from the nock crosses the bend in the bow. It is at this point that the greatest strain occurs and there is more pressing need for additional protection. Of this bow Murdoch says that "it approaches very close to the Arctic type, but shows traces of the Western model in having the ends of the long strands stretched across the bend and one single short strand returning to the tip from beyond the bend, while a fourth is precisely of the Arctic type, with a very large number of strands." The ivory levers shown upon the plate have been described, and are used in Cat. Nos. 2506 and 89466, U. S. N. M.

Figures 25 and 26 illustrate a peculiar "clove hitch" and "soldier's hitch" employed in this example.

Point Barrow. Collected by U. S. International Polar Expedition.

PLATE LXXIV.

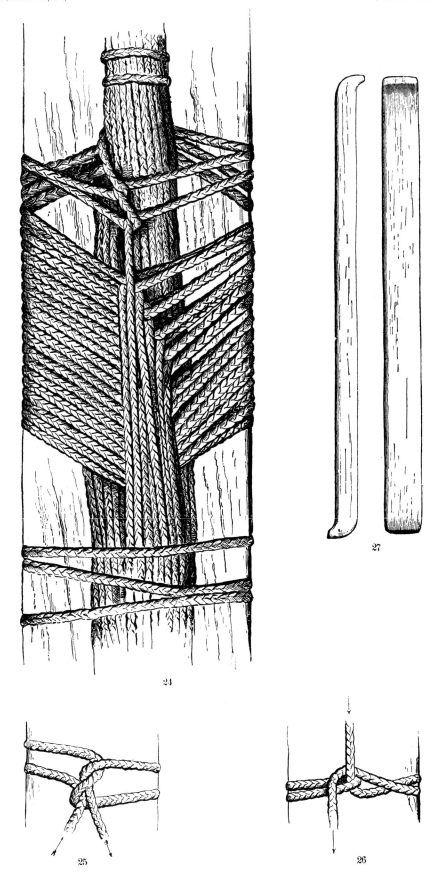

SINEW-BACKED BOWS OF ESKIMO, MIXED TYPE
(After Murdoch.)

TWISTING LEVERS FOR SINEW-BACKED BOWS OF ESKIMO.

This plate shows the manner in which the ivory levers are used in winding up the double cable on the back of an Eskimo bow. It will be seen that each lever has a hook at each end, but on alternate sides. The end of each lever is thrust through the middle of a loose cable, hook side downward. It is then revolved through half a circle, as far as it will go, then pushed its entire length, which brings the hook at the other end in place for another half turn, and so on. A rawhide string is passed through both cables, wrapped about the grip and made fast. This prevents the cables from unwinding while the bow is in use.

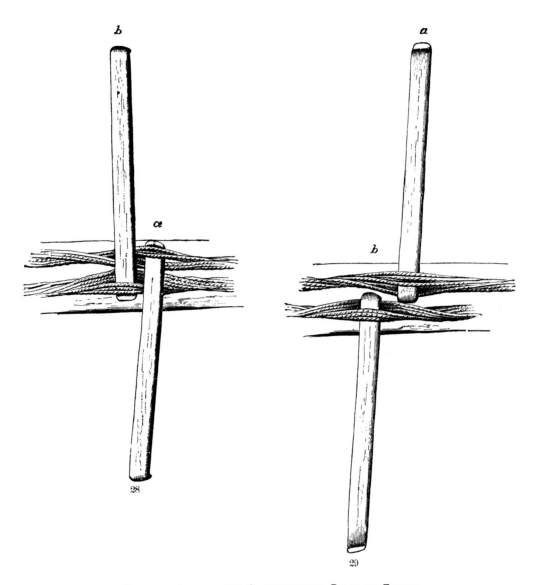

TWISTING LEVERS FOR SINEW-BACKED BOWS OF ESKIMO.
(After Murdoch.)

ARCTIC OCEAN.

Pt. Barrow, A.

Wainwright's Inlet A.

Mackenzie R. A

Siberia. W. & A.

Pt. Hope. A.

Kotzebue Sd. A.?

Bering St.

Diomedes. A.

Kaviak P or. A.?

Sledge Is.

C. Nome.

St. Lawrence Id. W.

Norton Sd. A. & S.

Yukon R. A & S.

C. Romanzoff. S.

Kus-koquim, S.

Nunivak Id.
S.

Bering Sea

Kadiuk Id. S.

Seal Ids.

Bristol Bay

Gulf of Alaska.

Aleutian Ids.

MAP
TO SHOW THE DISTRIBUTION OF THE
Eskimo Bows.

A. Arctic Type
S. Southern Type.
W. Western Type.

EXPLANATION OF PLATE LXXVII.

APACHE ARROW CASE AND ARROW.

FIG. 1. QUIVER, deerskin, smoke-tanned; bow case wanting. Arrow case, long tapering sack, stiffened at the back by means of a rod of wood sewed on with buckskin string. Decorated along the back and around the margins with scallops cut in red flannel and skin. A narrow band of exactly the same pattern is painted down the outside, directly opposite and around the upper margin. Bandolier, simple string of buckskin attached to stiffener. Filled with typical reed-shaft arrows, with hardwood twig foreshafts and iron points, as shown on the right of the quiver. Length, 35 inches.

Cat. No. 21515, U. S. N. M. Apache Indians, Athapascan stock, Arizona. Collected by J. B. White, U. S. Army.

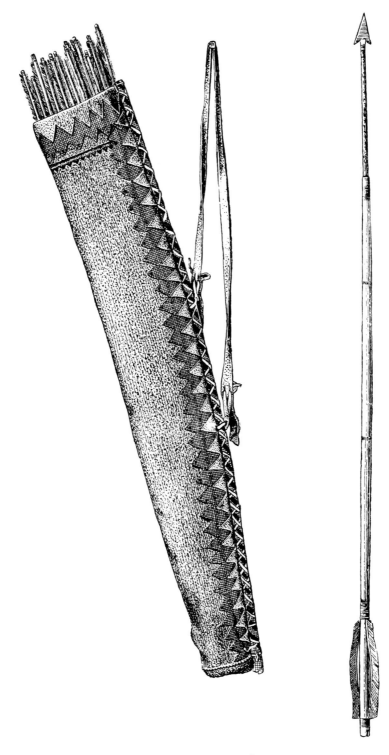

APACHE ARROW-CASE AND ARROW.

EXPLANATION OF PLATE LXXVIII.

APACHE ARROW CASE AND ARROW.

FIG. 1. QUIVER, deerskin. Bow case, none. Arrow case, bag with a stiffener of wood attached by means of strings along the seam. About the middle of the quiver is a band of smoked deerskin leather, with a fringe characteristic of the tribe, in which the scallop before mentioned appears. The bandolier is a strip of cotton cloth and blue flannel. Length of quiver, 34 inches.

Cat. No. 17331, U. S. N. M. Apache Indians, Athapascan stock, Arizona. Collected by Dr. H. C. Yarrow, U. S. Army.

NOTE.—The arrows accompanying this quiver, of which an example is given, are of the characteristic Apache type, shaft of reed, foreshaft of hardwood, points of iron. The extra length of the quiver is due to the fact that the reed arrows are longer than those with shafts of hard wood.

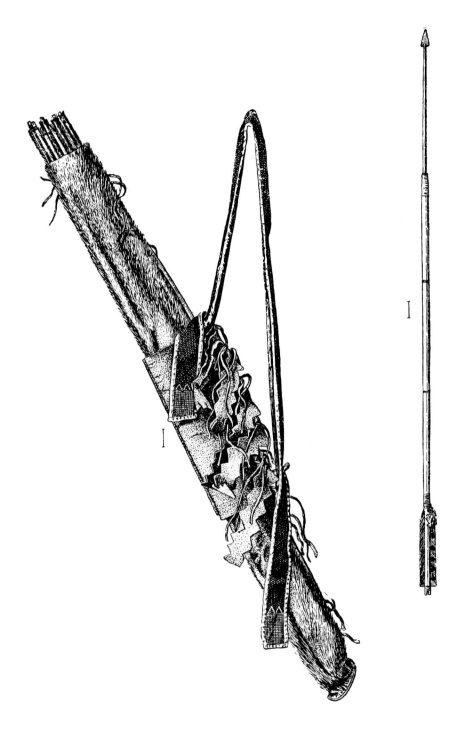

APACHE ARROW-CASE AND ARROW.

EXPLANATION OF PLATE LXXIX.

Navajo Quiver, Sinew-Lined Bow and Arrow, all of Northern type.

Fig. 1. Quiver, mountain lion skin. Bow case made with hair side inward; arrow case, hair side outward. There is also between the two, where they are joined, a stiffener of wood, which belongs especially to the arrow case, showing that the bow case is an afterthought. For decoration the ends of the bow case are adorned with a fringe of lion skin, and from the top of the arrow case the tail of the lion depends. Length: bow case, 44 inches; arrow case, 28 inches.

> Cat. No. 76684, U. S. N. M. Navajo Indians, Athapascan stock, Arizona. Collected by Dr. Washington Matthews, U. S. Army.

Fig. 2. Bow, made of mesquit wood, rounded on the back and oval in form, lined with sinew, which is strengthened by three bands of sinew. The grip is seized with a delicate wrapping of buckskin string. The ends of the horns of the bow are wrapped with sinew and there is no especial modification of the ends for receiving the string. The bowstring is of two-ply twine, sinew cord. Length, 3 feet 11 inches. The Tacullies or Carriers of British Columbia, the Hupa of northern California, and the Navajo of Arizona, all Athapscans, use the sinew-lined bow.

> Cat. No. 76684, U. S. N. M. Navajo Indians, Athapascan stock, Arizona. Collected by Dr. Matthews.

PLATE LXXIX.

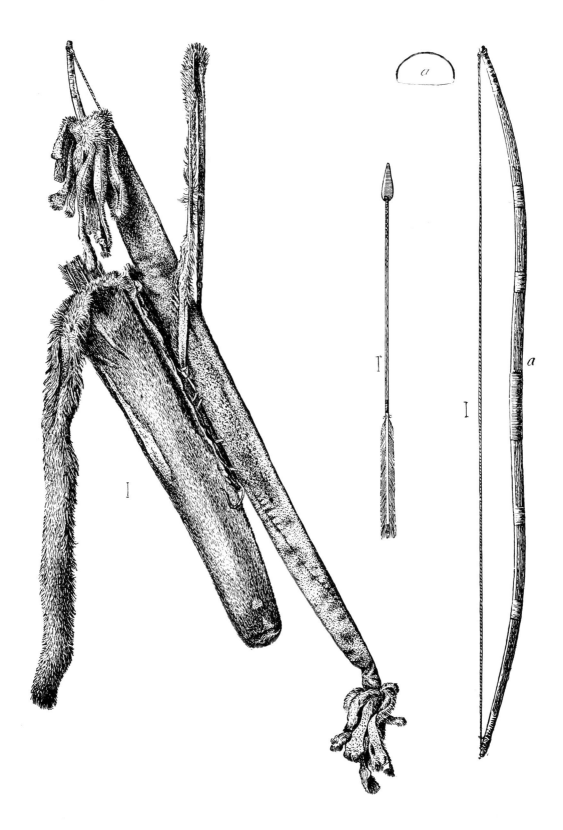

NAVAJO QUIVER, SINEW-LINED BOW AND ARROW, ALL OF NORTHERN TYPE.

EXPLANATION OF PLATE LXXX.

CHEYENNE QUIVER, SELF BOW AND ARROW, WITH SHAFT GROOVES.

FIG. 1. QUIVER, mountain lion skin. Bow case and arrow case separate. Both made with hair outward, and ornamented with fringes. From the bottom of the bow case depends one of the feet of the lion with claws. At the bottom is another foot of the lion wrapped with a red flannel cloth and slightly decorated with beads. Arrow case fringed at the top and bottom with strips of hide, and with a long pendant from the upper border made of the lion's tail, faced with red flannel and decorated with beadwork and ribbon. A unique attachment to this quiver is a streamer consisting of one and a half yards of red and black calico sewed to the inner lining of the arrow case. Bandolier, of lion skin faced with tent cloth (cotton duck). The bow shown in the plate with its arrow is of the form common throughout the Plains of the Great West. It is made of ash, and has a slight double curve. Length: bow case, 40 inches; arrow case, 25 inches.

Cat. No. 129873, U. S. N. M.   Cheyenne Indians, Algonquian stock.   Collected by H. M. Creel, U. S. Army.

PLATE LXXX.

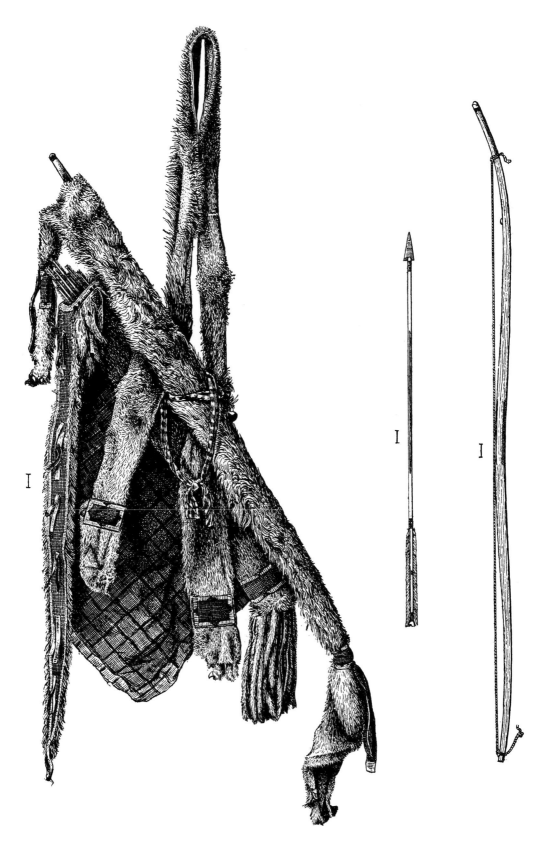

CHEYENNE QUIVER, SELF BOW AND ARROW WITH SHAFT GROOVES.

EXPLANATION OF PLATE LXXXI.

Chippewa Self Bow, Arrow, and Quiver.

Fig. 1. Bow, nearly rectangular in section, tapering toward the end; slightly double curve. One notch at each end and both on the same side of the bow for receiving the string, which is a 2-ply twine. Length: 3 feet 9 inches.

> Cat. No. 9063, U. S. N. M. Chippewa Indian. Algonquian, Dakota. Collected by Dr. W. H. Gardner, U. S. Army

Fig. 2. Quiver, dressed buffalo hide. Bow case is a long narrow sack, fitting bow; arrow case, wide bag tapering toward the bottom. Both ornamented slightly with fringe of rawhide, beads, and red flannel. The bandolier is a narrow band of buffalo skin with the hair on. Length: bow case, 38 inches; arrow case, 24 inches.

> Cat. No. 9063, U. S. N. M. Chippewa, Algonquian stock, Dakota. Collected by U. S. War Department.

Note.—The Chippewa Indians are more civilized than their neighbors, and this specimen shows a degenerate style of doing their own work, and much borrowing from the whites. The arrow is of the common Plains type.

PLATE LXXXI.

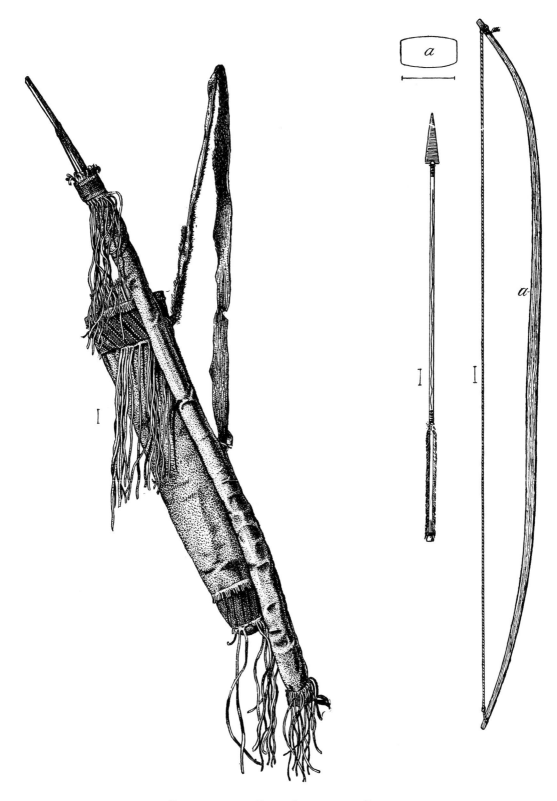

CHIPPEWA SELF BOW, ARROW, AND QUIVER.

KIOWA QUIVER CONTAINING BOWS AND ARROWS IN THEIR CASES, FIRE BAG, AND
AWL CASE.

FIG. 1. QUIVER, harness leather. The bow case is a long slender bag just fitting the
bow; the arrow case is a broad bag—both fringed at the bottom by cutting pieces of leather into strings. The two pieces are attached at the
margins with buckskin strings. Bandolier is a broad strip of rawhide.
The bottoms and upper margins of the bow case and quiver, the awl case,
the end of the bandolier, and the bottom of the tool bag are decorated with
leather cut in fringes. Length of the bow case, 44 inches; arrow case, 20
inches.

Cat. No. 152895, U. S. N. M. Kiowa Indians, Kiowan stock. Collected by James
Mooney.

FIG. 2. BOW, made of Osage orange. It is rounded on the back and inside, and
square on the sides. Largest at the grip and tapering along the limbs
toward the ends. The notches for the bowstring are cut in on alternate
sides near the end. The bowstring is made of 4-ply sinew cord. Double
curve. Length: 4 feet 4 inches.

Cat. No. 152895, U. S. N. M. Kiowa Indians, Kiowan stock, Indian Territory. Collected by Jas. Mooney.

This is a complete archery outfit. The bow case, arrow case, tool bag, and awl
case are separate. The bow is made of Osage orange. The bowstring is
of 4-ply twine or sinew cord; the arrows are of the original Plains type.
Shaft of hard wood, worked down with straight shaft streaks.

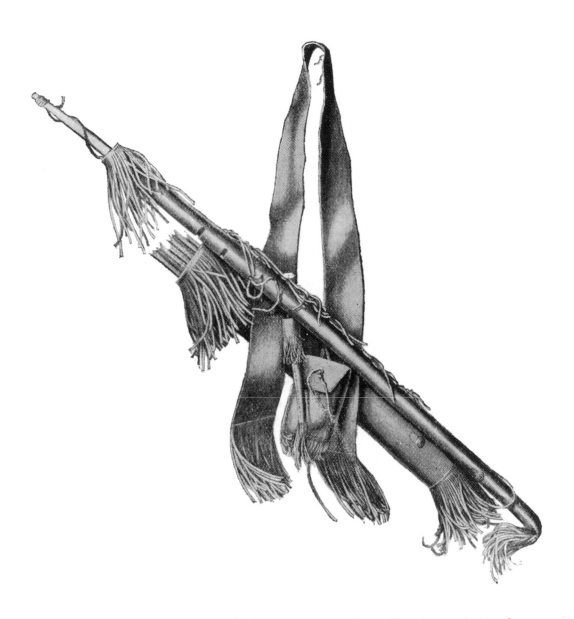

KIOWA QUIVER CONTAINING BOW AND ARROWS IN THEIR CASES FIRE BAG AND AWL CASE.

EXPLANATION OF PLATE LXXXIII.

DAKOTA QUIVER, SELF BOW AND ARROW, WITH SHAFT GROOVES.

FIG. 1. Bow, hickory, rectangular in section, double curve, tapering toward the ends. Two notches at one end, and one at the other for receiving the string, which is a 2-ply twine of sinew.   Length : 3 feet 7 inches.

> Cat. No. 131356, U. S. N. M.   Sioux Indians, Siouan stock, Dakota.   Collected by Mrs. A. C. Jackson.

FIG. 2. QUIVER, made of dressed buffalo hide.   Bow case and arrow case separate. The former, a long narrow bag; the latter, a short sack, slightly tapering toward the bottom.   Both are ornamented with rings of bird quill whipped on closely; the upper borders and the ends ornamented with finely-cut fringe.   The bow case and outside sacks, top and bottom, decorated with patterns in beadwork.   Length : bow case, 38 inches ; arrow case, 24 inches.

> Cat. No. 131356, U. S. N. M.   Sioux Indians, Siouan stock, Upper Missouri.   Collected by Mrs. A. C. Jackson.

The noticeable points on the arrow are the sinuous shaft streaks, the dainty feathering projecting behind the nock and the flaring nock, which gives a perfect grip for the thumb and forefinger in the shooting by primary or secondary release.

PLATE LXXXIII.

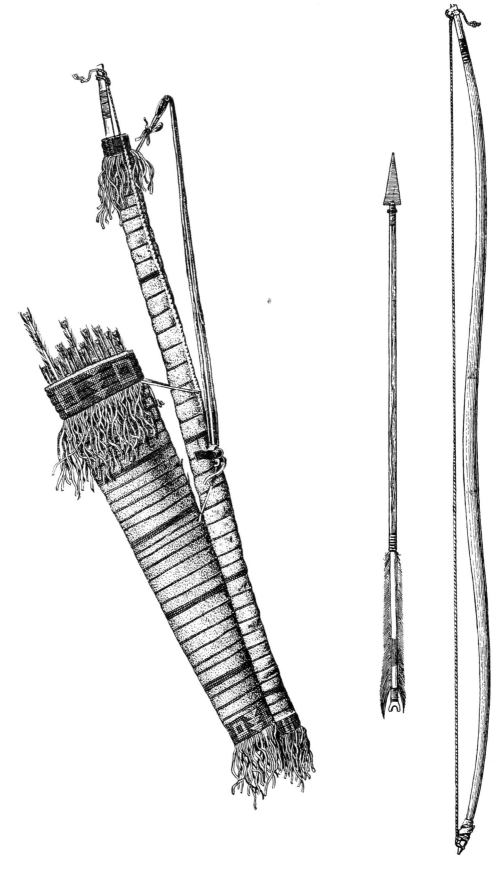

DAKOTA QUIVER, SELF BOW, AND ARROW WITH SHAFT GROOVES.

EXPLANATION OF PLATE LXXXIV.

SIOUX QUIVER, MADE OF COW SKIN, ARROW AND BOW.

FIG. 1. QUIVER, mottled cow skin. Bow case and arrow case are made after the usual pattern, ornamented at the top and bottom with fringes of hide with the hair on, and joined together by their margins. Bandolier of a strip of hide with fringes at the end. Length of bow case, 43 inches; arrow case, 26 inches.

Cat. No. 154016, U. S. N. M. Sioux Indians, Siouan stock, Dakota. Collected by Gen. Hazen, U. S. Army.

PLATE LXXXIV.

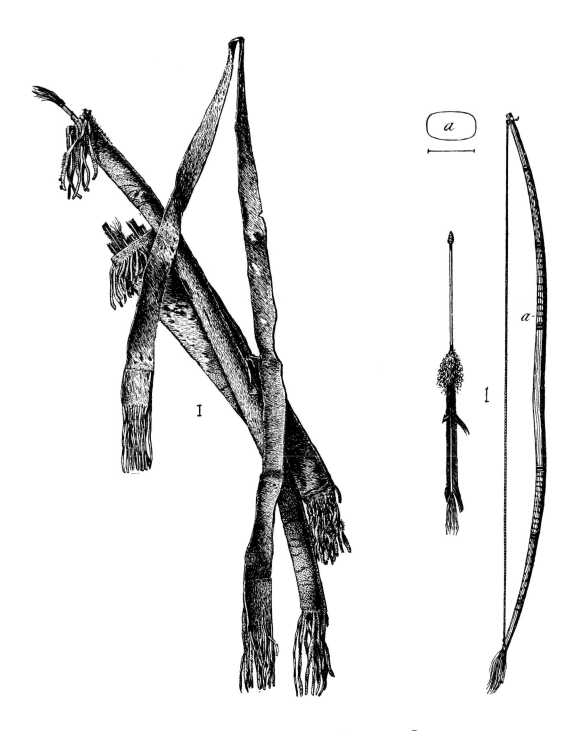

SIOUX QUIVER, MADE OF COWSKIN, ARROW, AND BOW.

EXPLANATION OF PLATE LXXXV.

DAKOTA QUIVER, SELF BOW AND ARROW, WITH STRAIGHT SHAFT GROOVE.

FIG. 1. QUIVER, of buffalo skin; bow case and arrow case separate. Bow case, a narrow bag just fitting the bow. Arrow case, a wide sack tapering toward the bottom. Both cases adorned at upper and lower margins with long fringes of buckskin, at the head of which is a band of red flannel decorated with "white-man's" patterns in beadwork. Bandolier is a strip of buffalo skin with hair left on. The bow and arrows are of the universal Siouan type. Length of bow case, 42 inches; arrow case, 26 inches.

Cat. No. 23735, U. S. N. M. Sioux Indians, Siouan stock, Dakota. Collected by Paul Beckwith.

PLATE LXXXV.

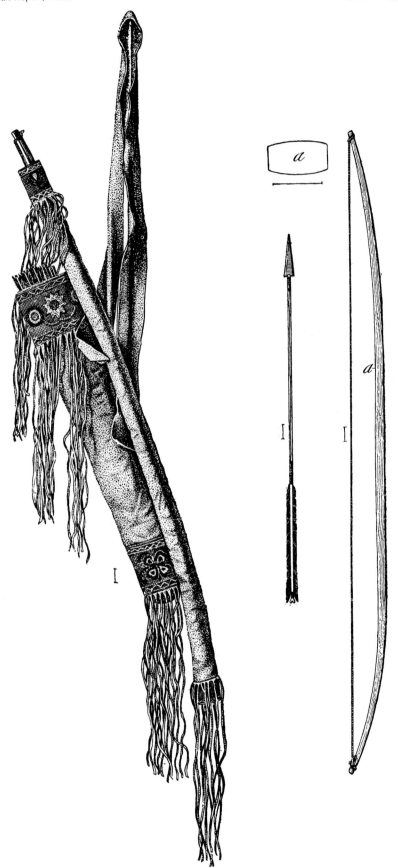

DAKOTAN QUIVER, SELF BOW, AND ARROW WITH STRAIGHT SHAFT GROOVE.

EXPLANATION OF PLATE LXXXVI.

TONKAWA.

FIG. 1. QUIVER, made of cow skin; bow case of mottled cow skin with the hair left on, forming a long close sack. The arrow case is a short, wide sack. Bandolier, broad strip of cow skin. From the ends of bow case, arrow case, and bandolier fringes of cut skin depend. The bow case and arrow case are sewed together at the margins or raw edges so that in the completed quiver the seams turn inward and are largely concealed. The tool bag is of rawhide and, singularly enough, contains a flint and steel and a powder charger made of the top of a buffalo horn. Length of bow case, 48 inches; arrow case, 28 inches.

> Cat. No. 8448. U. S. N. M. Tonkawa Indians, Tonkawan stock, Texas. Collected by H. McElderry, U. S. Army.

NOTE.—After the Government entered into a treaty with the Indian tribes, among the annuities were cattle, and from that time cow skin very largely took the place of other hides in the making of quivers along the Plains of the great West, where buffalo and deer were less abundant. Numbers of Siouan, Caddoan, Kiowan, Algonquian, Shoshonean, and Tonkawan tribes, all made their quivers of cow skin, either with the hair left on or tanned. The bow case and the arrow case were made after the general plan of the example here described.

FIG. 2. Bow, hard wood, hickory, the natural surface of the wood on the back. Section nearly square, tapering slightly toward either end. Notch single on alternate sides. Bowstring of 4-ply twine. Bow has a single curve. Length: 3 feet 11 inches. The arrow is of the Plains type, showing that region and game override social and other anthropological distinctions.

> Cat. No. 8448, U. S. N. M. Tonkawa Indians, Caddoan stock, Texas. Collected by H. McElderry, U. S. Army.

PLATE LXXXVI.

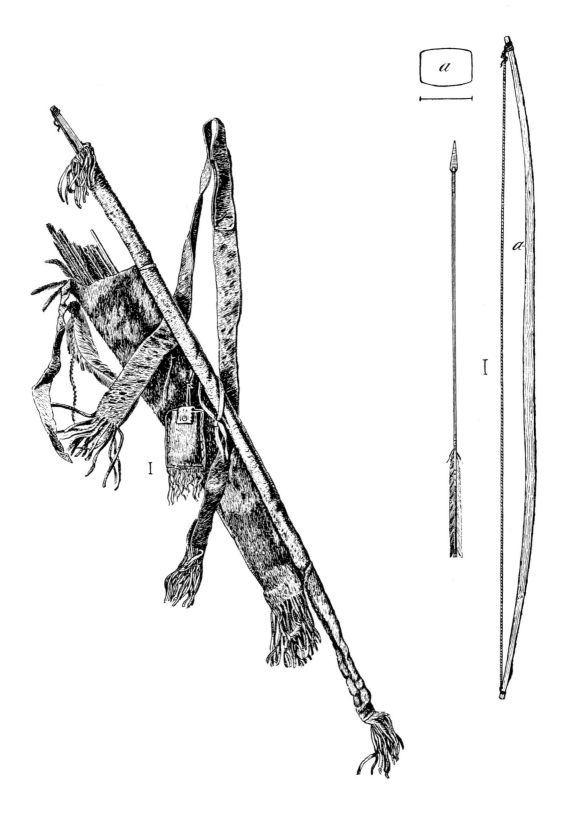

TONKAWA.

EXPLANATION OF PLATE LXXXVII.

SHOSHONEAN QUIVER, PLAIN ARROW WITH SHAFT GROOVES, AND SINEW-LINED BOW OF CALIFORNIA TYPE.

FIG. 1. QUIVER, black bear skin, with hair left on; bow case and arrow case separate. The ornaments are tassels of ermine skin hanging from the ends of the bandolier, and long flaps of bearskin, lined on the outside with green cloth and decorated with beadwork, ribbon, and gull feathers. The patterns on the green cloth are copied from those of the whites. Length of bow case, 41 inches; arrow case, 27 inches.

Cat. No. 9044, U. S. N. M. Snake Indians, Shoshonean stock, Idaho. Collected by Dr. S. Wagner.

FIG. 2. Bow, said to be Snake Indian bow from Idaho, but it belongs to the broad variety of sinew-lined bows of California. If used by the Snake Indians it has been introduced as a matter of trade. The nocks are simply tapering at the ends and no provisions for the bowstring, which is simply caught over the tapering ends. Same as 19322. Length: 3 feet 4 inches.

Cat. No. 9044, U. S. N. M. Snake Indians, Shoshonean stock, Idaho. Collected by Dr. C. Wagner, U. S. Army.

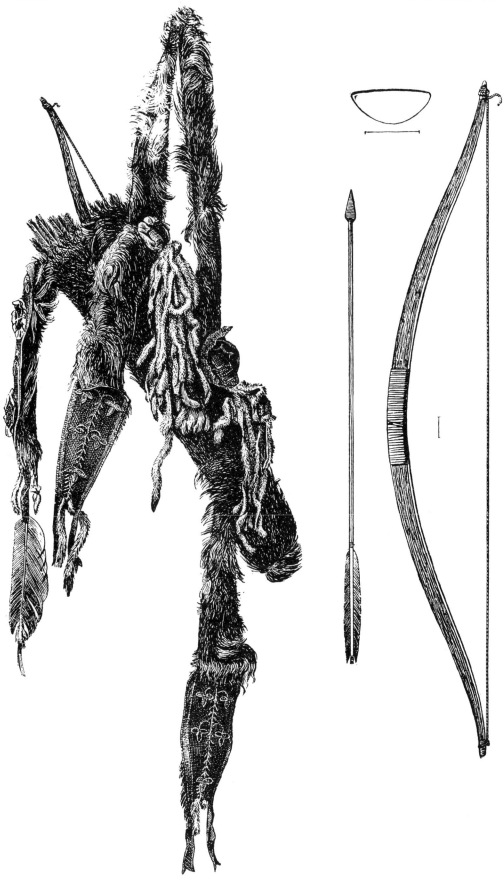

SHOSHONEAN QUIVER, PLAIN ARROW WITH SHAFT GROOVES, AND SINEW-LINED BOW OF
CALIFORNIAN TYPE.

EXPLANATION OF PLATE LXXXVIII.

Nez Percé Quiver and Bow.

Fig. 1. Quiver, of beaver skin; bow case and arrow case made separately of beaver skin with the hair side out. Ornamented at the bottom with tassels of strips of skin, bird feathers and little bells, and with bands of beadwork, and at the top with rings of beadwork and long flaps of beaver skin, lined with red flannel and decorated with beadwork. Bandolier missing. Length of bow case, 33 inches; arrow-case, 27 inches.

Cat. No. 23843, U. S. N. M. Nez Percé Indians, Shahaptian stock, Idaho. Collected by J. B. Monteith.

Note.—Tribes of the Shahaptian stock displayed a great deal of taste in all of their work, and some of the quivers from that region which are accredited to the Shoshonean and Salishan tribes have undoubtedly been made under the influence of these Indians.

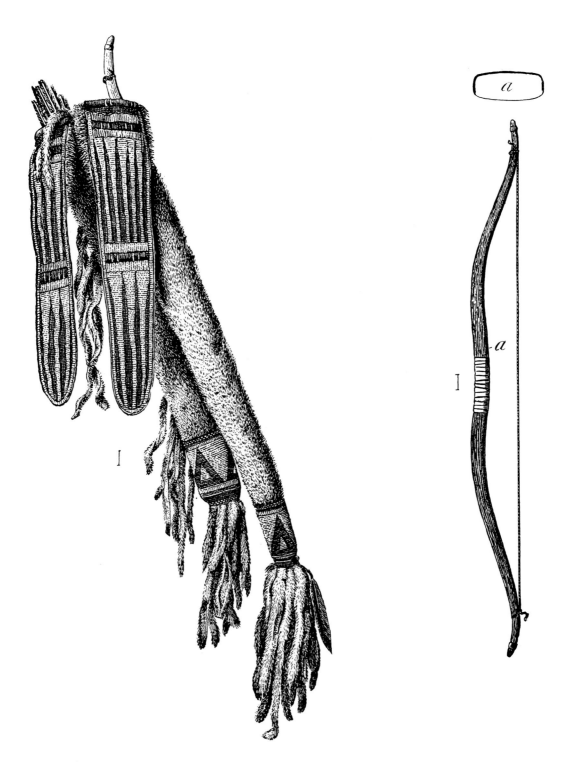

NEZ PERCÉ QUIVER AND BOW.

EXPLANATION OF PLATE LXXXIX.

UTE OR SHOSHONEAN QUIVER, BOW, AND ARROW.

QUIVER, deerskin; bow case, arrow case, and bandolier made of the same material, with the fur side outward. Adorned with fringes of the same skin cut in strips and with tufts of split feathers in which the stiff mid-rib has been removed. Length: bow case, 34 inches; arrow case, 28 inches.

Cat. No. 19843, U. S. N. M. Ute Indians, Shoshonean stock, Utah. Collected by Maj. J. W. Powell.

NOTE.—There is no tool bag, but depending from the top of the arrow case is a brush made of porcupine skin with the bristles left on. The bow is not sinew-lined, the arrow is of the universal Shoshonean type, and resembles those of the eastern Rocky Mountain tribes.

PLATE LXXXIX.

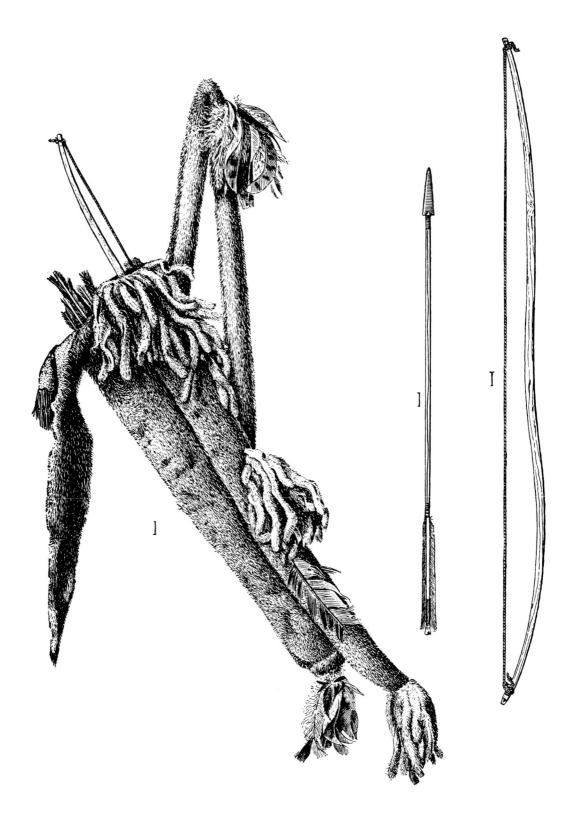

UTE OR SHOSHONEAN QUIVER, BOW, AND ARROW.

EXPLANATION OF PLATE XC.

Nez Percé or Shahaptian Quiver, Bow, and Arrow, with Sinuous Shaft Groove.

Fig. 1. QUIVER, otter skin; bow case and arrow case separate. Each of these is a narrow bag with the fur side of the bag outward. The bottom of the bow case has a broad band of buckskin with red flannel borders. The surface of the buckskin is covered with red, blue, green, and white beads in beautiful patterns. The bandolier is also of otter skin with a broad border of red flannel. On either side of the bandolier, and from the lower end of the bow case and arrow case, are long fringes made of strips of otter skin. The fringe of the bandolier is also adorned with a band of beadwork similar to that on the bow case. The upper border of the bow case and the arrow case are also decorated with beadwork, and long flaps of rawhide entirely covered with beaded patterns. This is a very beautiful object. Length of bow case, 20 inches; arrow case, 30 inches. Length of bandolier, 8 feet.

> Cat. No. 29886, U. S. N. M. Rocky Mountain Indians, tribe unknown. Collected by Dr. Fred. Kober.

NOTE.—A great many of the most beautiful objects in the National Museum were gathered by Army officers, who did not always know the exact tribe from which specimens were obtained. Quivers of this type are made by the Algonquian Siouan, Shoshonean, Salishan, and Shahaptian tribes of Montana.

PLATE XC.

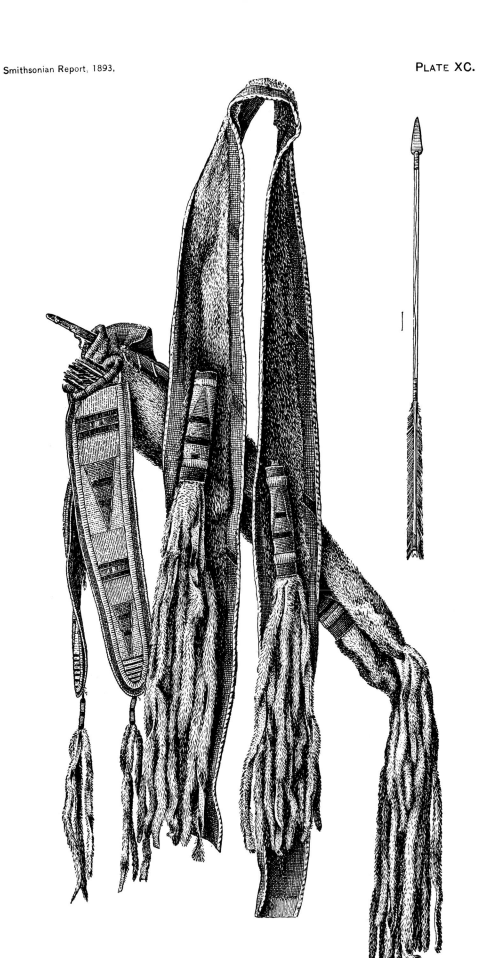

NEZ PERCÉ OR SHALAPTIAN QUIVER, BOW, AND ARROW WITH SINUOUS SHAFT GROOVES.

EXPLANATION OF PLATE XCI.

McCloud River (Cal.) Quiver, Sinew-lined Bow, and Foreshafted Arrow.

Fig. 1. Quiver, made of a whole deerskin with hair side inward. The skin of the legs has been left on and serve as pendants. The mouth is sewed up with buckskin strings and the ears protrude from the outside. There is no distinction between the bow case and arrow case. The whole forms a hide sack in which the bows and arrows are kept together. The bandolier is a mere strip of buckskin attached to the upper border and the middle of the quiver. Length: 40 inches.

Cat. No. 19322, U. S. N. M. McCloud River Indians, Copehan stock, Central California. Collected by Livingston Stone.

From this point southward the compound quiver disappears.

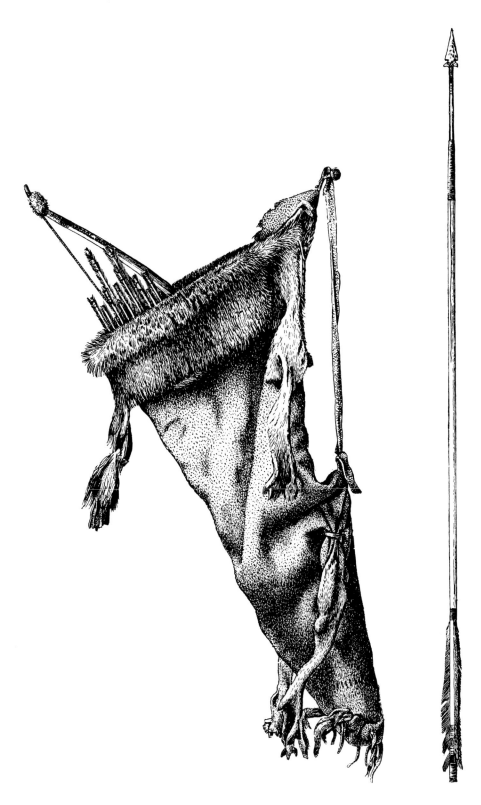

MCCLOUD RIVER (CAL.) QUIVER, SINEW-LINED BOW. AND FORESHAFTED ARROW.

EXPLANATION OF PLATE XCII.

Bow, Arrows, and Quiver of the Hupa Indians, of California.

Bow made of yew, broad and thin in the middle and tapering toward the ends, which are turned back. The nocks are wrapped with buckskin and trimmed with strips of otter skin. The back of the bow is lined with shredded sinew, laid on in glue and painted. The arrows have been described in the plate devoted to California types.

The quiver is made of the skin of the coyote, and is used as a bag for holding the bows and arrows. The method of finishing off the sinew at the end of the bow to constitute the nock and of fastening the bowstring is shown in the plate.

PLATE XCII.

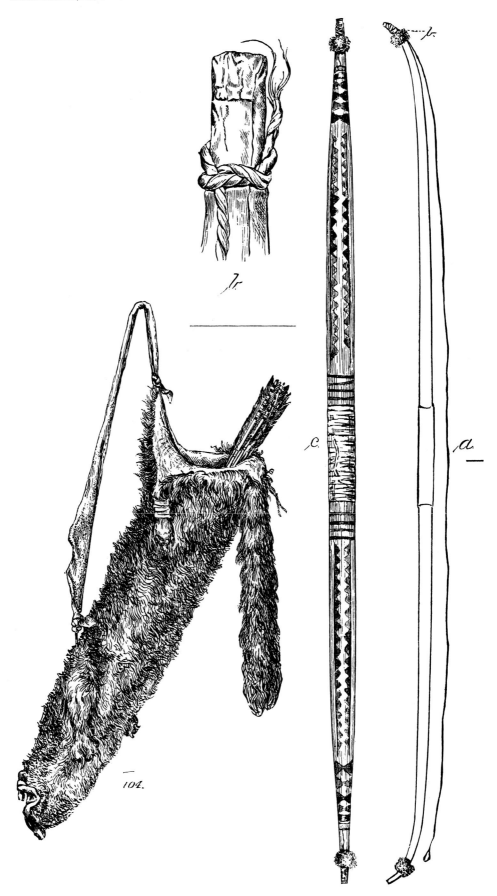

BOW, ARROWS, AND QUIVER OF HUPA INDIANS.

EXPLANATION OF PLATE XCIII.

CUMBERLAND GULF ESKIMO QUIVER, SINEW-BACKED BOW, AND TWO-FLAT-FEATH-
ERED ARROW.

FIG. 1. QUIVER, made of seal skin deprived of hair. The bow case and arrow case
are separate. Owing to exigencies of the sinew-backed bow the bow case
is very large, while the arrow case is very short. To the stiffener on the
back, by means of two thongs of rawhide, is attached a wire handle,
probably taken from an old pail. The bow case has a hood for inclosing
the bow. Length: bow case, 37 inches; arrow case, 25 inches.

Cat. No. 30015, U. S. N. M. Eskimo, Cumberland Gulf. Collected by W. A.
Mintzer.

It will be remembered that Mr. Murdoch calls attention to the greater simplicity
of the eastern Eskimo bows. Notice also the purely typical Eskimo flat feathers,
one on each side of the flat nock, made for the Mediterranean release.

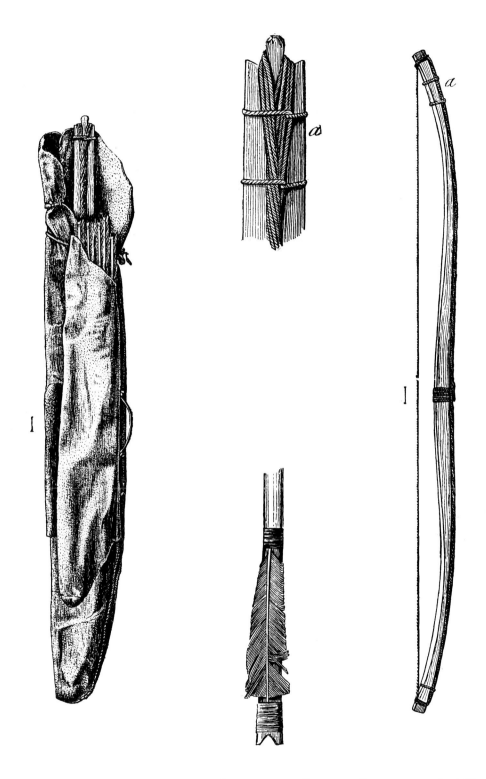

CUMBERLAND GULF ESKIMO QUIVER, SINEW-BACKED BOW, AND TWO-FLAT-FEATHERED ARROW.

EXPLANATION OF PLATE XCIV.

FORT ANDERSON ESKIMO QUIVER, SINEW-BACKED BOW, AND TWO-FEATHER BARBED ARROW.

FIG. 1. QUIVER (model); bag of deerskin without the hair. Made in the shape of an ordinary arrow case with a hood. Along the short margin is a stiffener of wood. Along the outer or longer margin are decorations made by suspending the false hoofs of the deer to short thongs of buckskin. Bandolier, simple string of rawhide attached to the stiffener. Length, 20 inches.

Cat. No. 7481, U. S. N. M. Eskimo, Fort Anderson, Canada. Collected by Robt. McFarlane.

NOTE.—This model of a quiver contains also miniature sinew-backed bow and arrows, but they are all correctly made in imitation of originals. Among the Eskimo, quivers of this form are very common and are long enough to contain the arrows and the bow within the hood.

PLATE XCIV.

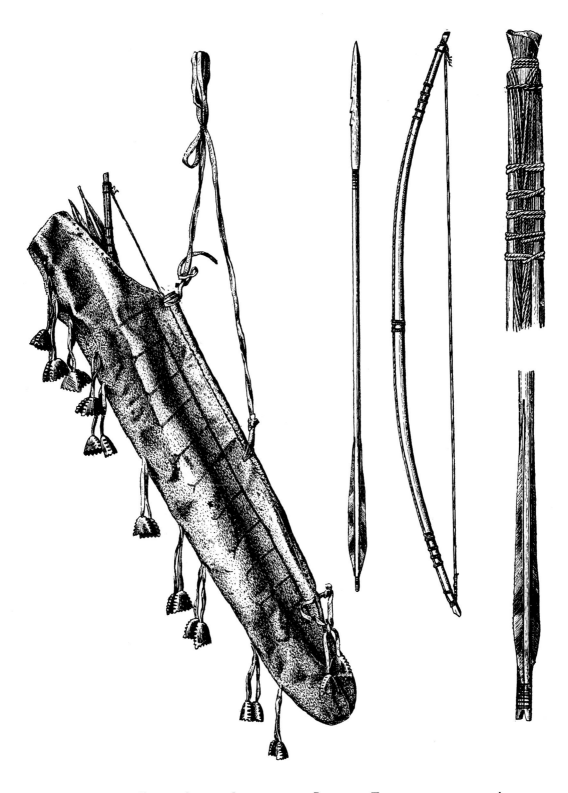

FORT ANDERSON ESKIMO QUIVER, SINEW-BACKED BOW, AND TWO-FEATHER BARBED ARROW.